D1492397

Dear
UNIVERSE

Dear UNIVERSE

200 Mini-Meditations for Instant Manifestations

SARAH PROUT

PIATKUS

PIATKUS

First published in the United States in 2019 by Houghton Mifflin Harcourt
First published in Great Britain in 2019 by Piatkus

9 10 8

Copyright © Sarah Prout 2019
Illustrations © Katelyn Morse 2019
Book design by Allison Chi

A CIP catalogue record for this book
is available from the British Library.

ISBN 978 0 349 42286 2

Printed and bound in Italy by L.E.G.O. S.p.A.

Papers used by Piatkus are from well-managed forests and
other responsible sources.

MIX
Paper from
responsible sources
FSC® C104740

Piatkus
An imprint of
Little, Brown Book Group
Carmelite House
50 Victoria Embankment
London EC4Y 0DZ

An Hachette UK Company
www.hachette.co.uk

www.littlebrown.co.uk

For the love of my life,
Sean Patrick Simpson

Contents

Part 1

HOW MY CONVERSATION WITH THE UNIVERSE BEGAN

"Intuition is a spiritual faculty and does not explain, but simply *points the way.*"

—FLORENCE SCOVEL SHINN

THE FIRST INKLINGS

felt intuitively when it was time to leave. It was the 31st of December, 2008. I had just turned 29, and it was another New Year's Eve that felt uninspired and underwhelming. My children were asleep, and so my husband and I watched a movie to celebrate the new year together. Max was perched in his "man chair" that his parents gave him for his 40th birthday. I sat on the red faux velvet sofa across the room. Being in our separate corners was often the safest option.

The movie was pretty terrible. I can't even remember what the title of it was. All I remember is that my husband blamed me for the poor choice and got angry because he wasn't entertained or amused. It didn't take much to trigger his anger. Over the ten years of our relationship, we didn't know how to be together and how to make one another feel whole and cherished. Sometimes, when I would use my voice and stand up for my needs, it would escalate to violence.

For the entire duration of my 20s, I felt so alone and isolated by the shame the violence in our relationship had created. The main reason I chose to stay was because I thought he would change. Max (not his real name, obviously) often promised me he would "get better" after our fierce and fiery exchanges. The power would sometimes shift faster than the weather patterns in Melbourne, Australia—which is where we lived at the time. It's often said that Melbourne has four seasons in one day, which is a perfect way to describe my marriage to Max. I would hold the power when he was in a state of remorse for lashing out and vice versa. It was a toxic cycle of forgiveness and forgetting

—like being trapped in a labyrinth. Both of us were unable to manage our emotions and guide our energy.

That particular New Year's Eve not only sparked anger, it was the perfect storm to give birth to the idea of change. After Max went to bed in a bad mood, I put on my fluffy white robe. I placed my iPod in my pocket and went out into the garden to watch the fireworks as it was approaching midnight.

I remember the cold feeling underneath me as I sat on the steps overlooking the kumquat tree in the backyard. In the distance I could hear people laughing and popping bottles of champagne. Music was playing loudly, and the occasional firework would explode. I felt so alone, so isolated, unseen, and unloved.

I put in my earphones to listen to some classical music. As midnight approached and I could hear people counting down, I began to cry. The tears were stinging my face as they rolled down my cheeks. In that exact moment I felt a sobering sense of clarity land in my heart, like I had just accidentally swallowed an ice cube. I looked upward to the sky, and I pleaded with The Universe:

Dear Universe,

Please take this pain away. I never want to experience another year of feeling lonely again. Help me find a way to change my life. Help me to leave here. Send me an inspired idea.

At that time in my life I had no money, very little confidence, or even the slightest clue how I would leave a ten-year marriage with two small children and start my life over. I had no idea that this moment of pain was such a powerful catalyst that it would help accelerate my desire for transformation. The truth is that when things feel painful enough, you are forced to create a new plan of action. However, leaving is never easy. On average, it takes a person who is trapped in an abusive relationship seven times to leave before staying away for good. Each attempt at exiting the situation is the most unsafe and unstable time.

I tried to leave at least nine times. When I finally built up the courage to leave Max, I walked away with over $30,000 worth of debt, two suitcases, and a heart full of hope for a brighter future. Let me tell you though, it was challenging! There were some days I didn't know how I would feed my children, because my welfare check kept us living below the poverty line. However, my newfound freedom felt so incredibly liberating. For the first time in my adult life, I felt peaceful.

If you would have told me then — at that exact point in my life — that ten years later I'd be living in Las Vegas with my soulmate, four children, and three dogs, and running a seven-figure business teaching people all over the world how to manifest their desires, I would have told you that you're probably crazy!

This is the extreme beauty of our lives — that the pain becomes a portal when you are ready to play with the energy of The Universe and remember your power to manifest.

CHOOSING LOVE OVER FEAR

We are sentient beings. This means we are hardwired to feel things emotionally. The times in our lives that call for transformation are based on taking actions on how we feel. In fact, most motivation for the reason we do something (anything in fact) is because our gut, our intuition, or our discernment guide us to draw a conclusion and act accordingly. We also tend to attach meaning to things through our own unique lens of life experience, whether it's through rose-colored glasses or viewing a glass as half empty.

Ultimately, whether you call the awareness of your emotions feeling, intuition, empathy, self-realization, or consciousness — we are the conduits for its actualization. There are hundreds of different types of emotions and feelings, and hundreds of words/labels for them that correlate with all sorts of different events that unfold in our lives. The spectrum covers everything from elation to feeling devastated. However, it all boils down to a choice in each moment, which is to either adopt a mind-set of separateness and disconnection (which is fear-based), or one of unity and togetherness (which is love-based). More simply put, you either remember that you have the power to guide your emotions and instantly manifest a new reality, or you forget and fall into a state of fear. The fear disconnects you from your infinite potential. It's kind of like when an Internet connection drops out. It cuts the cord and then invites you to rejoin the party again and again. It's a constant dance.

The important thing to remember is that you'll never choose love all the time. It's impossible, because fear and even negativity can serve a purpose to help you learn and grow. Being able to emotionally work with the less-than-desirable times in your life is such an untapped human superpower.

If we only remembered that we can guide this energy and trust that it's all part of the plan, forming a beautiful story, then the low points in our lives wouldn't seem so difficult or taxing.

The spiritual journey is all about remembering and forgetting.

This concept was taught to me by my very dear soul sister, Dallyce. She explained to me that it's perfectly fine to forget sometimes, as long as you remember that it's all a perfect part of a bigger picture and an integral part of the process. Sometimes there will be long phases and seasons of "remembering," and then there will be long seasons and phases of "forgetting." Her beautiful philosophy is that "it's all groovy" no matter what shows up.

The thing to remember is that you are the universe and you need to live your life as if it is happening through you instead of to you.

The three most important elements outlined in this book are to:

1. Rise above *fear.*

2. Embrace *love.*

3. Remember your *power.*

You'll do this through sparking a soulful conversation with The Universe, but first you'll need to accept your sacred invitation. Are you ready?

ANSWERING YOUR
SACRED INVITATION

I magine that an ornately patterned gold envelope has arrived in your mailbox. The embossed pattern is floral and almost otherworldly with intertwining decorative motifs that you instantly feel connected to. You lift the seal on the back to reveal the card inside that is addressed to you. It reads:

> Thank you for being here. This is your sacred invitation to begin your manifesting journey. You have the wisdom within you to remember our soulful union since the realm before time. Call upon me whenever you feel inspired to guide your energy. This will strengthen our bond and remind you of your power to create your own reality. Use meaningful mini-meditations to connect with this energy of superconsciousness to manifest your desires. It will enrich your life and spark the magical essence of limitless possibilities.

This is going to be a wild and exciting ride! Be still, and know I am here, I am YOU.
— The Universe

Most people only tend to "connect" to The Universe or God during times of crisis, just like I did during my New Year's Eve experience all those years ago. They attempt to invoke a higher power to ask for a miracle to manifest into reality. What I like to call "Dear Universe" moments usually happen when you find yourself at a crossroads, perhaps rock bottom, or riding a wave of uncertainty where the only seeming option left is to surrender to what is, be present in the moment, and hope for the best. Fear is usually the catalyst to seek support and divine guidance. You may tend to spark this sacred dialogue when you feel like all options have been exhausted, or you are nervously wishing with every fiber of your being for a successful outcome or transformation to take place to stabilize your emotions.

For instance:

Dear Universe, I need a miracle. Preferably now. Yesterday if possible! I promise I'll be a better person from this day forward if you make this happen.

We scramble to strike a bargain with a power outside of ourselves. However, it's only through sparking the connection with that power from within that the change can manifest instantly. These moments are defined beyond religious beliefs, practices, doctrines, and dogma. It transcends the color of your skin, your gender, sexuality, and political views and invites you to view life through a unified lens. Even though I studied meditation for many years prior to my own life-changing "Dear Universe" moment, I feel that reverence is something that needs to be consistently experienced. This is the golden thread that binds all of us regardless of which church, temple, mosque, gurdwara, or synagogue we choose to show up to. It's intentionally engaging with the power of superconsciousness and remembering where we originated from — the divine essence of limitless possibility. Whether you call it God, The Divine, Allah, Yahweh, Buddha, Source Energy, The Force, or The Universe*, the animating energy behind it all is the same. It's omnipotent, omnipresent, never-ending, formless, all pervading, and the unconditionally loving vibration of all that is and has ever been. This includes YOU and the journey your soul has traveled thus far to get you to where you are today. And this is why it's so important to get out of your head and into your heart to get curious about this tremendous field of potential. This same power holds the stars in the sky and keeps the water in the ocean.

* *There are many names and utterances for this Supreme Consciousness. For the sake of consistency in this book, I refer to it as "The Universe."*

FINDING ONENESS

Think about it for a moment — we are all made of the same stardust that the galaxies are comprised of. There are way too many unexplained phenomena in life not to believe that a bigger picture is at play. Things such as experiencing premonitions, near-death experiences, past life memories, ghostly apparitions, angel encounters, miracle healings, twin flame reunions, odd coincidences, and why baby pandas are so darn cute. The simple truth of these mysteries is that macrocosm equals microcosm. This means that everything in life is part of the greater whole, The Universe, and especially you.

There are so many things that occur in life with mystical significance that all succinctly point back to wholeness and Oneness. It would be virtually impossible for even the most hard-laced skeptic to quantify some of the great mysteries of life. For instance, and this is the big one, how the chances of actually being born as a human are so incredibly unlikely. Apparently winning the "human being lottery" is one in 400 trillion! With that realization alone, we are all winners and ultimately powerful creators. The precious nature of your incarnation is something to be treasured and deeply honored. We are all part of a much bigger picture than we sometimes realize or even remember. This is why, when life throws us unexpected situations, it's a little perplexing how we so easily lose sight of the divine plan.

LIVING ON A PRAYER

There are many masks and iterations of these "Dear Universe" moments and manifestations. They are the core essence of what defines the narratives of our existence. It covers such a broad spectrum of life experiences due to the different seasons and layers of awareness that reveal themselves along our journey. It's the mother who holds her breath waiting to hear the sound of her baby's heartbeat at the first ultrasound appointment. It's the husband who prays his wife will awaken from a coma after a terrible car accident. It's the activist passionately advocating for change in the eleventh hour. It's the schoolteacher who anxiously awaits the results of a biopsy. It's the couple keeping their fingers crossed that their mortgage application gets approved by the bank so they can finally buy their dream home. It's the single mother hoping her son stays out of trouble. Life is, and will always continue to be, full of many surprises, so you never know when your spirit will be called to rise up and call forth a miracle or a portal of connection in a "Dear Universe" moment.

Whether it's screaming out "Oh God!" when you're in the passionate throes of making love, to saying "Oh my Lordy!" when you change a poopy diaper that smells way worse than you anticipated, it's all an expression of soulful kinship. It's a call for support, community, authenticity, and deep reverence for connection to the divine within.

Feeling the full expression of emotions and connecting to The Universe is how deep meditation paves the way for transformation.

And to quote Bon Jovi:

"Whoa, we're halfway there. Whoa, livin' on a prayer."

But what if we use this power of prayer beyond moments of crisis, heightened physical or emotional states, and urgency? What would happen if we connected with The Universe daily and intentionally to conspire and create an amazing life of wellness, joy, peace, love, and abundance?

EVERYTHING IS ENERGY

One of the key reasons people tend to only consciously turn to The Universe in times of need is because they simply don't remember the power they have to create their own reality and ultimately manage their own energy. Sometimes we fall into a state of "spiritual amnesia," where we forget that we are part of a magnificent infrastructure of Oneness. That we have unlimited access to infinite wisdom all the time if we choose to tune in, tap in, and hone the innate superpowers that we are all born with.

The difference is in the understanding that you are here to remember that everything is energy and we are all connected. It's not about just marking time or treading water until we can shuffle off this mortal coil. I was reminded of this in a classic book by the 19th century New Thought writer, Ursula Gestefeld. She wrote: "Manifestation is the Purpose of Existence."

Indeed, this is a powerful truth because, as humans, we are reliant on things appearing in our reality in order to survive, thrive, and feel normal. We must manifest a roof over our heads, food to eat, water to drink, and people to love. These necessities are the product of intention, inspired action, manifestation, and ultimately being able to remember The Universe runs the show behind the scenes. We have the incredible ability to guide our energy to attract things, people, places, and experiences into our lives. If you're new to this concept, it might sound a little bit out there, woo-woo, or whack-a-doodle, but it's something called the Law of Attraction. It's a Universal Law that states that like energy attracts like energy. Or alternatively, birds of a feather flock together.

To simplify this, if you place anything under a powerful enough microscope, you will see that it's in a constant state of motion. Right down to the atomic structure — the protons, the neutrons, and the electrons are a buzzing energy of potential. Whether it's a rock, a dumpling, a piece of rose quartz, a silver fork, a Cabbage Patch doll from the 1980s, the sound of laughter, or a rainbow: It all has energy, it all is energy. People are no different and no exception. We all vibrate and oscillate at a very specific frequency. Thoughts

and especially feelings create our reality based on our vibration. I'll be sharing more about this throughout the book. Particularly how to guide your energy when you are feeling a certain way. I'll also be sharing some more personal stories and insights from my life and my work.

For more than ten years I've helped people all around the world to manifest their desires by sparking a consistent and sacred conversation with The Universe. I share my experiences from a space of service in the hope my messages will resonate within your heart.

THE DIVINE DESIGN

This book is a little like a Choose Your Own Adventure story. Feel free to flip through the pages and read the meditations in any order you feel called to. Trust that you'll be guided in the right direction at the perfect time.

The idea is that each mini-meditation is based on how you feel — or alternatively, how you wish to feel. After all, you construct the fabric of your reality based on your emotions and how you manage your energy. It's all about alignment. Each mini-meditation supports, guides, and meets you where you're at. This process will also help you to strengthen your levels of discernment and invite you to become more grounded in your feelings and ultimately strengthen your intuitive faculties. The goal is to give you a different perspective to try on.

You'll find that once you start to play with the energy of The Universe, you will begin to see radical, magical, and beautiful miracles show up and manifest in your daily life.

There are many themes and topics covered in the following two sections. The first section, "Rise Above Fear," helps to support you through times where you need a reminder to lift your spirits and be brave. The second section, "Embrace Love," helps you to celebrate and anchor the momentum you're building to manifest your dreams. It's a call to lead into love and possibility.

Listed are the top 100 fear-based feelings followed by 100 love-based feelings. Read and receive each meditation for the correlating emotion so that you can either move through it, or celebrate the essence of the energy to amplify your experience.

Please note: You need to be brave in order to see yourself clearly. Your commitment to transformation will be what gives you the strength to see beyond your current situation and remember the bigger picture. I offer various exercises or journal prompts to inspire you on your journey as you travel through the various feels.

I formulated the list of feelings intuitively. I pulled inspiration from psychology, mythology, New Thought ideas, and from my beautiful Manifesting Academy students who constantly remind me of the full spectrum of feelings that unfold on this inspired path. Some of the themes have also been based on my "Dear Universe" affirmations that have been shared millions of times on social media — so I know they help make a difference in the lives of others. More than likely, certain sections will resonate at different times in your life. I've written them holding the intention and heart-space that the story and guidance that accompanies each "Dear Universe" mini-meditation will hit home when it is needed at the perfect time over the course of your life.

This book is your sacred invitation for you to call upon the energy of The Universe and to remember your power. It's been designed to support you in your "Dear Universe" moments of need, but to also to spark "Dear Universe" moments to consciously create and manifest your own reality. In essence, it's a mixture of practical guidance, soulful exercises, personal insights, case studies, nuggets of wisdom, and potent prompts to enrich your connection to the divine within. Your role is to tune in to how you are feeling and then to take inspired action in whatever way you feel called to do so.

My wish for you is that when you learn how to guide your energy and your emotions that you will walk through a door into the next meaningful chapter of your life.

Let's now begin with a meditation of intention to get this party started:

Dear Universe,

May I now remember and connect with the highest and the purest source of divine energy. May we spark a sacred conversation, a soulful dialogue, to prompt deep and profound change from within to transform my life. My heart is open to all possibilities.
So be it, so it is.

Part 2

100 MINI-MEDITATIONS TO RISE ABOVE FEAR

When you practice self-compassion for whatever you're feeling, and you can consciously choose to guide your energy to a new space of empowerment, The Universe will show up in your current reality with unconditional love and support.

The fear-based emotion will move through your experience with ease and grace a lot faster when you are willing to pause and shine a light on the situation. If you are brave enough to get real with yourself, your pain will become an entry point for magical transformation.

The mini-meditations in this section will teach you how to ask The Universe for guidance, assistance, perspective, and wisdom. Sparking your connection to The Universe is the first step toward creating change and manifesting a new reality.

By not pushing your emotions to the side, or sweeping them under the rug, you allow yourself to invite powerful realizations to unfold. You authentically process your feelings from the most sacred space of awareness if you are open to finding resonance within a new perspective. You come to the beautiful truth that no matter what you are feeling, it ultimately serves a divine purpose.

You can rise above fear and embrace love because you remember the power of the present moment. This is compassion in action.

Each fear-based feeling listed will present a story, a nugget of wisdom, or a piece of inspiration followed by a "Dear Universe" mini-meditation to help you accept, release, or make peace with your current situation.

You'll also see a suggested list of three love-based mini-meditations, which you can turn to for inspiration. These suggestions are offered to guide you to a new space of emotional well-being.

Just remember . . .

WHATEVER YOU WANT is on the other side of fear.

Your experience is your own, and when you're ready, please tune in and ask yourself the following question:

WHAT AM I

feeling

RIGHT

NOW?

1. Abandoned	21. Defensive	41. Judged
2. Addicted	22. Depressed	42. Judgmental
3. Aggressive	23. Devastated	43. Lazy
4. Alienated	24. Disconnected	44. Lonely
5. Angry	25. Distant	45. Lost
6. Annoyed	26. Distracted	46. Mad
7. Anxious	27. Embarrassed	47. Manic
8. Ashamed	28. Empty	48. Manipulative
9. Betrayed	29. Enraged	49. Misunderstood
10. Blocked	30. Fearful	50. Moody
11. Bored	31. Flawed	51. Mortified
12. Broken	32. Guarded	52. Negative
13. Burdened	33. Guilty	53. Numb
14. Concerned	34. Helpless	54. Obsessive
15. Conflicted	35. Hopeless	55. Overwhelmed
16. Confused	36. Humiliated	56. Overworked
17. Controlling	37. Indifferent	57. Pained
18. Critical	38. Insecure	58. Panicked
19. Cruel	39. Irritated	59. Paranoid
20. Defeated	40. Jealous	60. Persecuted

61. Pessimistic

62. Powerless

63. Repressed

64. Resentful

65. Rigid

66. Sad

67. Scared

68. Selfish

69. Shocked

70. Shy

71. Sick

72. Stressed

73. Stuck

74. Suffocated

75. Suicidal

76. Suspicious

77. Tense

78. Terrified

79. Tired

80. Trapped

81. Traumatized

82. Triggered

83. Ugly

84. Uncertain

85. Ungrateful

86. Unhappy

87. Unheard

88. Unloved

89. Unsafe

90. Unsatisfied

91. Unseen

92. Unsettled

93. Used

94. Useless

95. Vulnerable

96. Wired

97. Withdrawn

98. Worried

99. Worthless

100. Wounded

① ABANDONED

DID SOMEONE YOU love and trust fail to show up when you needed them for support? Whether it's your spouse, your children, your parents, a colleague, or a friend, abandonment can manifest into a shape-shifting emotional monster if you forget the power you hold to guide your emotions.

Your heart might feel as if it has fractured into a million tiny pieces. It's a feeling of hollowness that can make your soul ache when someone leaves or distances themselves from your life. These wounds can be planted into your psyche from childhood, but the good news is that you can rewire your connection to the situation that triggers you.

Remember

YOU GET TO attach meaning to the events that unfold in your life.

The ongoing reality is that sometimes people don't show up in your life in the way that you expect them to. You might feel disappointed, hurt, or isolated by what you feel you're entitled to experience. The fear of being abandoned, or the experience of abandonment feels very real in the moment. It's the magnified energy of loss or the intense awareness that something has been taken from you — something that was never truly yours in the first place.

The truth is that you can never be abandoned if you remember the all-pervading love that The Universe has for you. Your soul story is always in the process of being written, and as real as it feels to allow your heart to sink into the space of victimhood, it's your call to rise up and remember your power.

You are never alone — you never have been, and you never will be.

Your experience of abandonment is an invitation to seek support and connect to a community of like-minded kindred spirits. People will always flow in and out of your life, and that's perfectly okay. Life is seasonal, and as you grow spiritually into this awareness, you can expect your pain to transform into a portal where the right people will always show up at the right time.

Let this be your meditation to shift your feelings of abandonment into excitement for the new people and soul family that are on the verge of appearing into your reality:

Dear Universe,

May I now remember your presence in my life so that I no longer feel alone or abandoned. In this moment, I ask that the energy surrounding the expectations of others is now released. I stand strong and inspired in my awareness that I am now attracting people into my life that support me, celebrate my success, and surround me with love. I am loved. I am cherished. **So be it, so it is.**

54: Loved • 85: Supported • 98: Welcomed

2 ADDICTED

ADDICTION IS WHERE love gets ripped apart and invites space for healing. If you are hooked on something that isn't serving you, this is your gentle reminder that you have the power to rise above it and release it when you are ready.

Living in Las Vegas has taught me to hold compassion on a new level for people who battle with addiction. I see mothers at traffic lights begging for money, trying to feed their babies. Homeless men holding cardboard signs in their dirty hands, barely able to keep their eyes open. Whether it's drugs, alcohol, food, sex, gambling, video games, cosmetic surgery, or drama, the full gamut of the human condition masquerading as suffering can be found in this crazy town in the middle of the Mojave Desert. Slot machines are in supermarkets, and billboards promoting women as consumables can be seen everywhere when you visit the famous Las Vegas Strip. This city showcases the highest of highs and the lowest of lows.

The truth? There is a tremendous beauty to rising above the judgment and seeing through and beyond the mask of sadness and self-destruction, no matter where you are in the world.

Remember

WE ARE ALL beautiful souls on a journey of self-discovery.

The sensitive and empathic people tend to take a detour to rip their hearts wide open and feel the fullness of the pain of life.

Being addicted to anything is a troublesome path that will remain in place until you can see the bigger picture at play. Your loved ones can try to help you, but until you are ready to take the necessary steps, then nothing will change.

One day at a time, one step at a time, one moment at a time, we can choose to guide our energy consciously. This is something to be incredibly grateful for. And for those we feel are lost, or if you feel lost for the time being, remember that The Universe has a plan. Love heals. Fear divides. And if you screw up? Choose again.

May this be your meditation to hand your addiction over to The Universe:

Dear Universe,

From this point onward I make the conscious choice to nurture and nourish myself. May I openly and graciously receive the help and guidance that is offered to me. I trust that my heart is healing and the energy of love is always with me. I have strength, courage, and wisdom to choose my path one moment at a time. One choice at a time.
So be it, so it is.

75: Safe • 82: Soothed • 85: Supported

③ AGGRESSIVE

WHAT'S GOT YOU so cranky? Being hostile or angry toward others is all about playing the blame game and making others responsible for your happiness. It's time to take ownership of this energy and channel it into a different direction. Take your power back! Your heart is in the right place, so there's no way you would intentionally wish harm upon another human being. Right?

Remember

THE AGGRESSION YOU hurl in another's direction will only result in harming yourself. It's like drinking poison and expecting the other person to die.

This is a beautiful opportunity to remember that the energy you put out there will always come back to you with astounding accuracy. Whether you've got steam coming out of your ears (cartoon style) because someone cut you off in traffic or you harbor feelings of hostility because your man won't leave the toilet seat down, it's important to realize that unmanaged emotions like these can become very toxic, very quickly.

It's often said that physiology changes your psychology and the way that you think. With that in mind, if you feel like you've got your cranky pants on, or you want to lash out and cause pain, step outside and move your body. Go for a run. Do some jumping jacks. Take a cold shower, and then bring your awareness back to the present moment. Now find five things to be grateful for, and then turn to this meditation as your guiding light to move through to a better space:

Dear Universe,

May I now inhale the energy of peace, of love, and of presence.
I exhale feelings of anger, aggression, and feeling antsy. I tune my focus to feel appreciation and I take ownership for the reality I create.
So be it, so it is.

10: Calm · 14: Compassionate · 35: Forgiving

ALIENATED

IF YOU ARE feeling alienated and are reading these words, it's more than likely you feel distant and separate from the people in the world around you.

You might have turned your back on your family and loved ones, or cut ties with certain friendships. Perhaps someone turned their back on you? The truth is that as humans we are wired to require connection in order to be healthy.

Remember

IF YOU ARE feeling isolated and alienated it's imperative that you seek support and reach out to someone who could lend a friendly ear.

In this moment, as you read these words, please visualize someone holding your hand and being there for you.

Invite the space in your heart to be open to this meditation:

Dear Universe,

Right now I feel alienated, but I'm willing to move through this experience to remember the importance of human connection. May I remember that my soul essence is sparked when I allow others to share my life. I set the powerful intention to welcome new friends and experiences that will bring me joy.
So be it, so it is.

16: Connected · 60: Nourished · 82: Soothed

⑤ ANGRY

ANGRY, HUH? YOU know the feeling. Your blood is on the verge of boiling because someone didn't behave in the way you expected them to, or things didn't go according to plan. It's time to let it out and let it go.

Remember

YOU CAN'T FEEL empowered if you are angry.

If anger isn't managed properly, it can manifest in less than desirable ways. My personal belief is that depression is anger turned inward that hasn't been dealt with or processed. This is why it's so incredibly important to shift your focus to things, people, places, and experiences that bring you joy. Rise above it!

Harboring the energy of anger is an opportunity to choose again, pick another card, pass Go, and collect $200. If something rattles your cage, thank The Universe for the invitation to move through the experience. This is way easier said than done, but once you learn how to forgive faster, you ultimately free up your energy field to receive more magnificent manifestations.

So here are two powerful questions for you:

- How expensive is it for you to hold on to the anger?
- Wouldn't now be a good time to let it go?

Once you feel ready, move into this meditation to release the anger and free yourself from pain:

Dear Universe,

I trust that the lesson within this experience is being revealed in perfect divine timing. May I now release any feelings of anger, negativity, and heaviness so that I may be brought back to a state of peace, of presence, and of joy.
So be it, so it is.

14: Compassionate · 35: Forgiving · 63: Peaceful

 **ANNOYED**

FEEL LIKE YOU have a short fuse right now? Are things that other people are doing really starting to tick you off?

When you feel the energy of irritation, please try and shift your focus to how you can show up in the present moment and be of service to others. One of the students in my Manifesting Academy wrote to me stating that she felt impatient and annoyed that nothing was manifesting for her. She asked me for the best way to help remove feelings of annoyance.

My suggested remedy was this:

I told her to go to the post office to buy a stamp when she knows it's going to be really busy. Her mission was to stand in the line where she would usually feel annoyed and to energetically send love to the people around her in her mind. When every tiny irritation would rise up, she would then shift her awareness to the loving energy she had to offer complete strangers. Within a week my student noticed the difference in how her levels of annoyance at the tiniest things had dissolved because of the 45 minutes she had spent in the post office. You see, when you feel irritated, the best thing you can do is look for things to appreciate and ask yourself what's great about your current experience. You can try this exercise for yourself at the post office, a busy supermarket, or even while stuck in traffic.

 Remember

SEE THE ANNOYANCE as an invitation to show up in the present moment.

To dissolve your own levels of irritability, allow this to be your meditation:

 *Dear Universe,*

I release feelings of annoyance and switch them to the
awareness of things around me to appreciate. May I see irritation as a
cue to look inward at what can treasured in the present moment.
So be it, so it is.

36: Free · 67: Present · 71: Relaxed

7 ANXIOUS

AS A CHILD, I would worry about everything. I was scared of the dark, afraid of people, fearful of food, terrified of change . . . and the list goes on! My anxiety would manifest as nail biting and mentally obsessing about the unknown. Most people are anxious about things that haven't happened yet. They are fixated on a detail they believe will unfold in the future and steal their happiness.

Remember

TUNING IN TO the present moment and taking a deep breath will help you to feel calm.

The best way to steer your anxiety to a space of feeling grounded is to take one moment at a time and to trust that The Universe is looking after you.

Allow this meditation to alleviate your concerns for the future:

Dear Universe,

I am safe. My anxiety is an illusion and an invitation to guide my energy to a space of presence. So I move my awareness to hopefulness and excitement for what I am in the process of manifesting.
So be it, so it is.

10: Calm · 15: Confident · 43: Guided

8 ASHAMED

I STOOD UP out of the bed, kissed my lover on the forehead, and put my clothes back on. As I left his apartment, I called my husband to say that I would be home late for dinner because I was catching up with a friend. I lied. For the first time in ten years, I had slept with another man. The pain was so bad in my marriage that I was desperate to find an escape path. Little did I know that lying and cheating would leave me feeling so ashamed. Even though I resented my husband, Max, for the years of abuse, I just couldn't justify that I had betrayed him in this way.

Sometimes in life, we do things that we're not proud of.

As humans we make mistakes, and those mistakes can haunt us for years on end. I know it did for me! Then one day, after the dust settled, I could see purpose in the pain I had created.

Remember

WE ARE NOT the sum of our mistakes. We're not even the same people we were when we took a so-called wrong turn.

The transformation takes place in the understanding that we can always choose a better way. Keep in mind this awareness doesn't give you a golden ticket to continuously make bad choices; however, seeking forgiveness begins with self-forgiveness.

Allow this meditation to help release the manifestations of shame in your life:

Thank you for the awareness that I am able to choose a path of integrity. May I now lovingly release the past, forgive myself, and move forward into a reality that never intends harm on another human being.
So be it, so it is.

35: Forgiving · 36: Free · 91: Unashamed

⑨ BETRAYED

THE ENERGY AND essence of betrayal packs quite a punch in your heart. For some, the manifestation of pain can last for years. If you have been double-crossed, cheated on, taken for a ride, or led down the garden path, just remember that in time you may see it as a blessing in disguise.

Remember

TRUE COLORS ARE always exposed. This situation is The Universe doing your soulful housekeeping on your behalf.

Allow The Universe to help heal your heart and remind you that there is a beautiful purpose in this painful experience. It might not make sense right now, but it will in time.

Dear Universe,

May I release any feelings of negativity from my
body and my heart. I now forgive the past and put it behind me. I now
move forward into a future of honesty, integrity, and joy.
So be it, so it is.

35: Forgiving · 40: Gracious · 47: Honest

BLOCKED

MORE THAN LIKELY, you will feel blocked at various points in your life, and it's perfectly okay. It can be so frustrating to feel as if your usual flow of inspiration has come to a complete standstill. Your energy might feel like you're on low battery mode and you feel unmotivated to see the bigger picture at play. When we feel blocked, it's because we need to invite space for inspiration to be presented in a different form or way. You need to mix up your energy a bit. Perhaps go for a walk, take a bath with Epsom salts, brew a hot cup of tea, and remember that sometimes feeling blocked is a great opportunity to incubate trust that The Universe is gathering the information you require to prompt you to take inspired action very soon. Think of it as an intermission that builds momentum behind the scenes to create a new level of awareness.

Remember

IF YOU FEEL blocked, please see it for what it is, and don't make it worse than it is! Too often we make mountains out of molehills, as the old saying goes. Meditate on this and ask The Universe for some gentle assistance when needed:

Dear Universe,

I am ready to take inspired action to jump back into the flow of energy that serves me. May I release any blockages and trust that my mojo will return when I feel rested and refreshed in perfect divine timing.
So be it, so it is.

13: Clear · 58: Motivated · 61: Open

 # BORED

MY NANA MOLLIE was one of the most creative and artistic women I have ever met. Born in 1913, she was hired to draw fashion illustrations for magazines in the early 1930s. Near the end of her life, her house was filled with beautiful portraits she had painted. There were incredibly detailed faces of the Maori indigenous people of New Zealand, women who had inspired her, and the youthful and vibrant faces of her many beloved grandchildren. For my seventh birthday, she presented me with a portrait of my Cabbage Patch doll, which I still cherish to this day. Each set of eyes hand-drawn or painted expressed her artistic gift to capture the creative essence of the present moment.

In a time before the television, the Internet, social media, smart phones, and Netflix, the concept of boredom meant that you had too much time on your hands.

My nana told me that I was not allowed to be bored and that it was an opportunity to be creative. My mother carried this philosophy into my childhood as well. I was allowed to use swear words, but I was never to utter the words "I'm bored."

Remember

THE BEAUTY OF inspiration is sparked from and a deeper understanding of who you are as a spiritual being.

Feel bored? Draw, write, read, walk, cook, listen, unplug, and reset. Also, meditation helps tremendously . . .

Dear Universe,

I surrender to the feeling of boredom. I trust that it serves
a purpose to ignite creative energy within my soul.
So be it, so it is.

⑫ BROKEN

YOU MIGHT FEEL broken right now, but you can never truly be broken. Despite your circumstances, there is purpose in feeling the way you do right now. In time, it will all make sense, and the purpose will be revealed.

To give you an example, from 2013 to 2015, my body felt completely broken. The week before I married my soulmate, Sean, in Las Vegas, I suffered a miscarriage at six weeks. In the space of just eight short months, I lost five babies in total. We fell in love with the tiny heartbeats, at various stages, only to discover that they weren't going to make it. The doctors were puzzled as to why this kept happening and why I was becoming pregnant so regularly and easily at the age of 33. I felt like my body was failing me because I couldn't keep my babies alive. As a manifesting teacher, this experience tested my faith at the highest level and rattled my belief in The Universe.

How could I serve people if I felt so broken?

During this time, I was extremely open and vocal on social media about my experience of loss. Pregnancy loss, by the way, needs to be more openly expressed in society since as many as one in three pregnancies results in miscarriage.

What I came to realize during this time is that sharing my story and being vulnerable was actually helping to inspire people on their own journey. Together, through seeking support while feeling a little broken, we sparked the healing energy of community.

By the time I held my miracle baby, Lulu Dawn, in my arms in 2015 I had been pregnant for a total of 18 months! It was almost like the gestational period of an Asian elephant! My point here is that sometimes you need to ride out the illusion that you are broken as a way to strengthen your life's mission and purpose.

Remember

THE UNIVERSE WILL always test you, present you with a painful narrative to rise above, and never give you more than you can handle. You just have to hold faith in the process and prepare yourself for the wild ride.

Please meditate on healing feelings of brokenness within to lean into the beauty of wholeness . . .

Dear Universe,

Allow me to see this time in my life as a valuable learning curve. May my heart receive the nurturing energy it requires to move through this experience with ease and with grace.
So be it, so it is.

8: Brave · 29: Expansive · 99: Whole

⑬ BURDENED

FEELING A LITTLE weary right now? Take comfort in the fact that life is seasonal and you will move on from this in time. Feeling burdened in different areas of your life is completely normal. Whether you feel the sting of not being able to pay your debts on time, or you have to care for a sick loved one — it takes some serious inner-game work to transform the gravity of the heavy energy into light.

When I left my first marriage, I left with less than nothing. I had $30,000 of crippling credit card debt and no way on knowing how I would ever be able to pay it back. With two children to take care of, my welfare checks each week left us with very little money for food — let alone debt repayments! The bank would call me and ask for money at least four times a day. I prayed for them to stop and ended up manifesting the disconnection of my phone service because I couldn't pay the bill! With no washing machine, no fridge, a banged-up old car, a cheap roof over my head, pee-stained thrift store mattresses for the kids to sleep on, and not much hope for a stable financial future, I felt the full-scale burden of fear. Panic attacks, stress, and anxiety were my mode of operation. Then one day, something my mother shared with me helped to radically transform my mind-set:

"Just take one day at a time."

And that's exactly what I did. I would celebrate each milestone of getting through the day. I would feel grateful for the loaf of bread and beans that the kids could eat.

Remember

FEELING BURDENED IS an invitation to get fully present. One moment to the next you can rise above it and into a new and stress-free reality.

My daily meditation went a little something like this:

Dear Universe,

Thank you for the opportunity to train in the fullness of life.
I am open to your guidance and to receive inspired ideas and actions
to move forward through this experience.
So be it, so it is.

36: Free · 71: Relaxed · 90: Trusting

14 CONCERNED

FEELING CONCERNED ABOUT someone or something? It's perfectly natural to feel concern from time to time, as long as you're not crossing boundaries with other people. Sometimes you might express concern over someone else's behavior. Perhaps they are drinking too much, not exercising enough, or not seeking the help that you think they need.

More than likely your concerns are based on your own set of rules, beliefs, and values. However, if you are genuinely worried or anxious about another's welfare, then you have a duty to offer help and support where appropriate.

Remember

THE UNIVERSE REVEALS to you constant clues of how you can show up and be of service. The key is to offer support without judgment. This is true compassion.

Another thing to remember is that if it's none of your business then you need to stay in your own lane.

Dear Universe,

May I trust that all is well and unfolding as it should in the right way.
I now release the need to control others and believe in the journey.
May my concerns be transformed into faith.
So be it, so it is.

15: Confident · 40: Gracious · 61: Open

15 CONFLICTED

IT'S ESTIMATED THAT at least 35 percent of all romantic relationships now begin online. This means you can fall in love with anyone from anywhere around the world. I met my husband, Sean, on Twitter! We were on opposite sides of the planet, which created several complications. We were tweeting for about a year, soon we became Facebook friends, and then moved to email. It was like a light switch was flipped, and we fell in love, even before we met one another in person! Sean used all of the money he had in the world to fly to Australia from Los Angeles for 11 days to visit me. During that time we knew we wanted to be together forever, but our lives were both in turmoil. As a single mother, I just couldn't afford another mouth to feed. However, we were determined to find a way.

After the 11 days, Sean and I decided on a trial of three months together to see if we could build a life as a couple. We argued, we laughed, we cried, we dreamed, and at the end of the three months, Sean promised me that he would return. The one element I found disturbing is that he took all of his stuff with him. He was conflicted to the core of his being.

Taking the leap of faith to be with me meant that he had to leave his home in America. Everything he had ever known would need to be left behind. His heart felt torn between the woman he loved and the life he was comfortable with.

Remember

YOUR HEART WILL guide the way, and there are no mistakes or wrong turns. Your soul craves adventure. Feeling conflicted is your higher self inviting you to leap out of your comfort zone.

If you feel conflicted and you're not sure which direction to head, please meditate on this:

Dear Universe,

May I now be guided from within to choose the path that serves the greatest good. I trust that there are no wrong turns, just valuable experiences that help my soul and heart to flourish and grow.
So be it, so it is.

13: Clear · 71: Relaxed · 89: Transformative

16 CONFUSED

YOU MIGHT BE feeling a little confused right now. What if I told you that there is beauty in not knowing all of the answers to your questions? You're in this delicious discovery stage of peeling back the many layers of awareness in order to understand what is unfolding. It's a miracle, if you choose to see it this way.

Remember

CONFUSION IS THE call from your higher self to seek clarity and go with the flow.

Allow The Universe to help you out when you need assistance to untangle your rainbow Slinky of emotions during this time . . .

> ### Dear Universe,
> I trust that I will be guided and receive answers to my questions when the time is right and not a moment sooner.
> **So be it, so it is.**

13: Clear · 43: Guided · 86: Surrendered

CONTROLLING

IF YOU CAN identify that you're being controlling, then more than likely it's because you have a specific set of rules, and someone (or yourself) is breaking those rules. The opposite of being controlling is being free. How do you feel when you think of switching out the control for freedom? Tune in to the energy of how it will feel when you release all of the expectations you have around yourself and others. It must feel magnificent.

Recognizing that you are being a "control freak" is a call from The Universe to let go and to surrender. People who are really good at manifesting and being in the beautiful flow of life are willing to let go of the reins and relax a little. After all, what's the worst thing that can happen? The constant burden of perfectionism is the fastest way to make sure that you never feel fully relaxed.

Remember

WHEN YOU EXERT control, you turn your back on the trust you have in The Universe.

It might seem like a super-scary thought to realize that it's time to let go of the need to control things, but if you want to be happy, you must release this behavior that is definitely not serving you. The good news is The Universe is always there to support and guide you when you feel the need to control others.

Dear Universe,

May I now release the desire and the need to control others.
I now trust and surrender to the idea that everything is unfolding
as it should, with your divine guidance.
So be it, so it is.

17: Content · 71: Relaxed · 86: Surrendered

⑱ CRITICAL

MY DEAR FRIEND and first meditation teacher, Bhai Sahib Ji, was an elderly Sikh gentleman from Malaysia. He would wear a beautiful lilac-colored turban, and he had a long flowing white beard. He traveled the world teaching people about the bridge between science and spirituality — which was often met with the mind-set of disbelief. When he visited Australia, he would stay with Max and me. In the evenings, we would sit and drink tea, and I would ask him questions about The Universe, metaphysics, alchemy, and humanity.

One piece of wisdom that he gave me was this statement that I treasure dearly: "Criticize me all you want, take my karma."

The concept of karma is essentially that the energy you put out there will return to you. Bhai Sahib Ji believed that when a person is critical, they take on the energy of the thing they are criticizing. To simplify this concept, imagine that each time you leave a negative comment, review, or judgment on a blog article or social media post, that the energy of the criticism you are expressing will return to you.

Whether you believe in karma or not, this philosophy can empower you to reflect on the need for expressing criticism. It's an opportunity to channel your energy in a direction that will serve you the most.

So when you're feeling critical, take a moment to pause and reflect on the energy you are putting out there.

Remember

COMPASSION OVER CRITICISM is the path of love and least resistance. Also note that constructive feedback can be very helpful if you are invited to express your opinion.

Meditate on this to release the tendency to criticize others:

Dear Universe,

I now choose to guide my energy toward the truth of the matter.
May I remember the connectedness and Oneness of humanity. I will hold my tongue when my heart shows me that I cannot improve upon the conversation.
If it is not an expression of kindness, it is not necessary.
So be it, so it is.

14: Compassionate · 29: Expansive · 76: Satisfied

19 CRUEL

IF YOU ARE willfully causing pain or suffering to another, or feeling no concern about it, then you need to check yourself. There is no reason to be cruel with your words or your actions.

A Buddhist saying reminds us to filter our words through this list:

Is it truthful?

Is it kind?

Is it necessary?

When we lash out and say something that we know will cause harm we are almost always doing it because we don't feel very good about ourselves. I've done it myself many times when I have verbally cut someone off at the knees. Usually I know where their pain points and sore spots are, so I give myself full permission to be cruel. This is a terrible trait to have. However, if you can recognize it, then you can shine a light on it and stop it from happening. I am fully committed to healing this tendency within my psyche to master the art of nonviolent communication. It's a gift to have the awareness to speak words of kindness.

Remember

SPEAK THE WORDS that will contribute to your relationship rather than contaminate it. Cruelty is a symptom that your heart needs some self-nurturing.

Dear Universe,

Allow me to resolve conflict as it arises with compassion,
nonviolent language, and words that are fair. I now choose love over poison,
to allow the pure beauty of consciousness to blossom.
So be it, so it is.

14: Compassionate · 42: Grounded · 97: Vulnerable

20 DEFEATED

GEORGE WAS A homeless man who I walked past on my way to school every day. He kind of looked like Oscar the Grouch from Sesame Street. In fact, he smelled like he lived in a trash can too. He would only ever have two things with him: beer and a blanket. The word around town was that he used to be a millionaire, and he was so defeated by his financial loss that he chose to leave his family and live on the streets. George would yell at people and demand that they buy him beer. As far as he was concerned, the world had defeated him and owed him something. He would pee in the doorways of the local stores, he would yell abuse at people, and he would sleep wherever he wanted to. He just gave up. Rock bottom was the place he remained, until the day a bus hit him and killed him instantly.

Remember

THE UNIVERSE WILL never give you more than you can handle.

With this awareness you can never truly be defeated by your circumstances. During our times of suffering, we forget that no one gets out of their earthly experience alive. We're all going to shuffle off back into Oneness sooner or later.

If you feel defeated, remember the power of perspective and to connect to The Universe to guide you during this time . . .

Dear Universe,

Remind me that I am on my way up and my current experience is a valuable lesson. Thank you for this opportunity to grow and this gift of awareness that life is seasonal.

So be it, so it is.

17: Content · 33: Flowing · 51: Inspired

21 DEFENSIVE

I ATTENDED AN event called Engage from Your Stage to learn how to master the art of public speaking — which terrified me at the time! Over the course of four days, we were taught how to construct the perfect "signature talk" to share our messages with the world. First we had to deliver our talks to the attendees of this particular event. Our instructor asked us to meet all feedback without responding and to not get defensive or to make excuses. This experience was intense! After I spoke for ten minutes from the platform, I had to listen to the honest feedback of my peers.

"You were pacing too much."

"Your eye contact was only on the left side of the room."

"Your forehead wrinkles when you make a point and it looks a little scary."

For every comment I felt defensive. And then I decided to let it go and just listen. I decided not to take it so personally.

Remember

SOMETHING MAGICAL IS unlocked on the other side of your defensiveness.

If you can stand in stillness and observe, rather than defend your situation, you will find great strength.

The next time you are trying to deflect the truth or not allow space for growth, please ask The Universe to help you move through the experience:

Dear Universe,

Allow me to stop defensiveness in its tracks. May I see the situation as a gift to rise above egotistic concerns and trust that there is a divine plan in the process of unfolding.
So be it, so it is.

4: Aware · 29: Expansive · 50: Inquisitive

22 DEPRESSED

IF YOU'RE FEELING depressed, please know that you're not alone. There are 350 million people worldwide who experience depression. After a woman gives birth, there is also a 10 to 15 percent chance that she will develop postnatal depression. I've been through this twice — after the birth of my first child and my fourth child. The feeling of depression is like you have a wet blanket wrapped around your head and your heart. The perception of your reality is foggy, hollow, and empty. With that being said, only you can define how it feels for you.

I have a theory that depression is the result of unprocessed feelings over time. Purely on a metaphysical level, there is a block in the flow of energy.

Remember

YOU ARE A powerful, energetic being. Life is flowing through you all the time if you allow it.

Another important thing is to be kind to yourself and take one day at a time. The emotional fog will lift when it is meant to move on. In the meantime, you must trust that this experience is forming part of your journey.

Ask The Universe for guidance, seek support, talk to people who can help, and remember that life is seasonal and more than likely you won't feel like this forever . . .

Dear Universe,

I ask that this experience be lifted, so that I may feel vibrancy in my heart and trust that these feelings are part of my journey. You cannot see the light without darkness. Once I remember the contrast, please allow the feeling of depression to be released. I am happy, whole, and healed.
So be it, so it is.

44: Happy · 45: Healed · 99: Whole

23 DEVASTATED

I LOOKED AT the ultrasound screen and saw my baby all curled up with precious little arms and precious little legs, all perfectly formed . . . but without a heartbeat.

"I'm sorry," the technician said.

My entire being began to collapse into an energetic sinkhole. Time stood still. I can't even remember what he said next, or what I said to him or the nurse in response. I just remember throwing my clothes on and storming out of the hospital as fast as possible. I was 16 weeks pregnant and only 20 years old. I felt devastated that my baby had died within me.

Even though I gave birth to a healthy baby boy the year after my first loss, I still felt the full force of the emotional devastation. I needed support and to recover from the trauma.

When something devastating happens in your life, it's important that you don't allow it to define you.

Remember

THE UNIVERSE WILL quite often teach you how to get comfortable with uncertainty in order to bring you back to the magic of the present moment.

If you are feeling devastated by something bad that has unfolded in your life, please remember to connect to The Universe and try this meditation:

Dear Universe,

I trust that you will reveal the purpose of this pain in time. May I remember that this emotional season will pass and I will heal when the time is right. In the meantime I am committed to self-care and self-compassion.
So be it, so it is.

54: Loved · 85: Supported · 100: Worthy

24 DISCONNECTED

LIFE CAN BE busy, crazy, random, overwhelming, and scary. If you're feeling disconnected right now, it's probably because your dial is set to look for the red instead of the green. It's such an easy trap to fall into. We all flitter (like a butterfly) between connection and disconnection at various times in our lives because it serves a purpose to remind us of the constant dance of possibility.

Remember

LIFE IS ALL about remembering and forgetting. It's cyclic.

When you feel disconnected from The Universe, people, and inspiration, you are in a phase of forgetting. It will pass. However, if you can identify that you are disconnected, remember to ask The Universe for help and guidance to remind you of how sweet it is when you are plugged back into the flow of magical opportunities:

Dear Universe,

May I remember that we are all part of the same fabric of Oneness.
I now seek connection through the things and experiences that bring me joy.
I can re-spark connection when my heart feels full.
So be it, so it is.

16: Connected • 29: Expansive • 67: Present

25 DISTANT

WHY ARE YOU feeling distant right now? Is it because you feel disconnected from your loved ones? Your spouse, perhaps? In most cases, if you are feeling distant then you are also being perceived as being distant. If it's not your intention to create space between you and your loved ones, then talk about it. Express how you're feeling and that it's not meant to be taken personally while you are taking a little time to get back into a state of balance and purpose.

Remember

YOU HAVE 100 percent permission to take time to process your emotions — whatever they are!

The danger exists in not being present with your life if you are feeling distant. Your role is to close the gap between fear and faith. Being far away emotionally means that you are harder to reach and connect to.

Dear Universe,

May I hold compassion for others around me.
May I express that it is not my intention to come across as distant. I trust that I am present with this process. I allow the solace I seek to create the healing within my heart that I require at this time.
So be it, so it is.

16: Connected · 55: Loving · 67: Present

26 DISTRACTED

DO YOU GET easily distracted from what you're meant to be doing? The average American spends 2.6 hours a day on their phone! Over the course of your lifetime that's a total of more than five years! It's more time than you will spend eating and drinking. Attention spans are getting shorter and shorter because social media gives us endless feeds to scroll through. We are exposed to thousands upon thousands of chunks of useless information on a daily basis. No wonder we get so easily distracted!

Remember

YOUR POINT OF power is in your ability to be still and aware in the present moment.

Challenge yourself to unplug for a little while each day. One of the biggest ways I have found to not get distracted and remember to focus on what's important is to get my phone out of the bedroom. I replaced it with an old-school alarm clock. This helps to cultivate presence and start the day off with intention. If you find it hard to focus and you get easily distracted, try this:

Dear Universe,

My energy is present in this moment. I am showing up
fully to participate in the task at hand. My energy is grounded and
purposeful. This is the essence of my soul's mission.
So be it, so it is.

33: Flowing · 34: Focused · 67: Present

27 EMBARRASSED

"HA HA! LOOK at how red Sarah is turning! She looks like a beet!"

I was eight years old. I was very shy and self-conscious. As the new girl in school, I had to stand up and introduce myself to the class. I could feel the heat rising in my face, flushing my cheeks. There was nowhere to hide from the embarrassment. Any time I would be asked to speak aloud, give an answer, or have the attention of others focused upon me, I would blush. I would blush, and the mean boys would have something to say about it.

The curse of this level of embarrassment has followed me around for most of my life. I can confidently speak to an audience of thousands, and it doesn't bother me. However, when a stranger compliments me on something, I blush. It doesn't happen all the time, but I'm still aware of it.

Things that unfold in your life that trigger the feeling of embarrassment are based on your own unique rules that have been broken. You might feel embarrassed because you called your new boyfriend your old boyfriend's name, in bed. You might have bent over and farted accidentally during a quiet moment at your child's school piano recital. You might have waved back at the person who was actually waving at the person behind you. Embarrassment can bring with it a lot of beautiful humor.

Remember

THE ABILITY TO laugh at yourself is so important. We are not the sum of our quirks or peculiar reactions. We are the sum of our courage to move through each moment with ease and grace.

I still go red from time to time. Big deal. Embarrassing situations arise. How we move through them and process them into our consciousness is what matters the most.

Dear Universe,

I feel embarrassed right now, but please remind me that one day none of this will seem important. May I laugh at this situation and find divine humor as a powerful teacher.
So be it, so it is.

53: Joyful · 64: Playful · 91: Unashamed

 # EMPTY

FEELING LIKE YOUR soul tank is running on empty? Just know and trust that it happens to everyone from time to time when we feel like we have nothing to give. This is why it's so important to fill up your cup, refuel your soul, and light up your heart so you can join the party and not miss a single moment of magnificent action throughout your life.

Remember

IF YOU BELIEVE you are empty, take action to fill yourself back up again.

The fastest way to remedy emptiness is to seek joy. Watch a funny movie, read a book, eat nourishing food, get some sleep. Do things that light up your soul. Allow yourself to be a little selfish and commit to doing nice things for yourself on a daily basis.

The Universe is always ready and waiting to fill you back up again when you make the request . . .

Dear Universe,

In this moment I visualize being surrounded in the nurturing energy of golden light. May I see this light entering into my heart and filling it with joy, laughter, love, and purpose. I am whole and I am healed.
So be it, so it is.

17: Content · 29: Expansive · 99: Whole

29 ENRAGED

WHEN I WAS 14, I had a horse named Cecil. He was pretty old, but I loved him dearly. I would ride him around our ten-acre farm and spend hours upon hours just being with him. Then one day someone left the fence open and Cecil escaped. In his mad dash for freedom he galloped up the road into oncoming traffic. He was hit by a small yellow Toyota Corolla, which broke his spine and legs. He died soon after.

The next day, the driver of the vehicle knocked on our door to apologize.

"You killed my horse, you bastard!" I screamed. I was enraged. I was so angry at this poor guy who had no clue that a horse would be around the corner.

When we are enraged by something, it's usually misplaced and unnecessary. The chemicals that our bodies create when we are furious at someone or something is toxic to our systems. This is why it's so important to pick your battles and spend your energy wisely.

Remember

IF YOU CAN guide your emotions to be nonviolent in your reactions, it's the most self-loving thing you can do.

If you feel enraged by something or someone, then turn to The Universe for your guidance in this moment . . .

Dear Universe,

Remind me of the power I have to guide my emotions. May I soften my reactions to peacefully speak my mind and express my truth in a kind, nonviolent manner.
So be it, so it is.

10: Calm · 35: Forgiving · 86: Surrendered

30 FEARFUL

IF YOU'RE FEELING fearful, imagine you are safe and protected. You are so much stronger than you think you are, and you will get through this time in your life. Being fearful is your call from The Universe to rise above your current situation and be brave. It's your soulful invitation to run toward your greatest potential.

The divine purpose of fear is to move you through your comfort zone. Anything magical and miraculous that happens in your life will manifest on the other side of facing your fear. This is why all of us are so scared by so many different things. We're scared of public speaking, heights, death, pain, crocodiles under the bed, spiders, loss, and most of all: uncertainty. We're afraid of not being in control. We're afraid that the future holds many unwanted and unfriendly surprises. We're afraid that if we do venture out of our comfort zones, we will get hurt.

Remember

YOU ARE AN extension of the power of The Universe. You can rise above anything challenging that manifests into your life. You can tune in to the energy of strength and always manifest bravery when you need it most.

Facing your fears will release you from the burden of concern — you will be okay, no matter what happens.

I once heard that a life lived in fear is a life half-lived. More often than not, our minds like to blow things out of proportion and worry about situations before they arise. Fear lives in the present moment when you don't trust The Universe. If you switch your thoughts to appreciation, celebration, and enjoyment, then it dissolves the fear as quickly as spoonful of sugar in a cup of tea.

If you feel fearful, allow The Universe to help you transform your thoughts to remember your opportunity in this situation . . .

Dear Universe,

I now release these feelings of fear and replace them with love
and trust that I am being divinely guided. May the fear fade away and
the love be illuminated within my heart.
So be it, so it is.

8: Brave · 43: Guided · 86: Surrendered

31 FLAWED

AFTER I LOST my first pregnancy at 16 weeks, I was painfully underweight. It was such a shock to discover that I was pregnant again just eight short weeks later. The doctor told me that I would have a better chance of keeping my baby alive if I gained a few pounds. For breakfast I would walk down to the store after Max went to work, and I would select food items to binge on. Three chocolate ice cream cones, a large bag of chips, candy, more ice cream . . . and the list goes on!

I was not only eating to gain weight, but I was eating to manage and stuff down my emotions. By the time I gave birth to my precious baby boy, I had gained nearly 70 pounds! It was a combination of stress, grief, sugar, and the manifestation of shame for being in an abusive relationship and bringing a child into that family dynamic.

My 21-year-old body looked radically different from the carefree teenager that I had been not so long ago. I also sustained a muscle separation due to the weight gain. My tummy looked like a crumpled paper bag or a deflated balloon. I felt so flawed! I had no idea at the time that this flaw was due to something so incredibly beautiful.

Remember

TAKE HEART THAT there is power in not rejecting parts of ourselves. Flaws are opportunities to remember our unique magnificence.

For example, kintsukuroi ("golden mend") is the Japanese art of fixing broken pottery using a process of lacquer resin that fills the cracks with gold or silver.

The philosophical significance is that in the fixing of the flaws, they become part of the object's design. It's believed that once a piece has been mended, that it is even more precious, valuable, and beautiful than before.

Meditate on your so-called flaws and imperfections and invite yourself to rise above the illusion of perfection . . .

Dear Universe,

May I now embrace all of who I am — in body, in mind, and in spirit. Allow the cracks in my consciousness to be filled with golden and silver light. I am so proud of who I am today and so grateful for this beautiful life experience.
So be it, so it is.

25: Empowered · 74: Reverent · 99: Whole

32 GUARDED

FEELING GUARDED MEANS that you've built a tiny (or giant) wall around your heart, and there is not much space for you to have an authentic connection with others. This belief that you must protect yourself from others probably stems from being betrayed — someone perhaps broke your trust. The flipside of this coin is that you might unconsciously see people as competition.

Remember

THE TRUE BEAUTY of human connection is to allow yourself to be seen.

Comparing oneself to others is often a reason people give themselves to feel guarded. It's so important to remember the old saying that comparison is the thief of joy. As cliché as it sounds, you must allow yourself to dance like no one is watching. You must love people with your whole heart. Live your life as if good things are constantly flowing into your reality. It's imperative to remove this energetic barrier and be open. If you don't? The Universe can't deliver your desires because there's a block in your flow.

If you feel guarded, allow this meditation to remove your resistance:

Dear Universe,

I now allow people, places, and exciting experiences to
flow into my reality. I trust with an open heart that I am guided and protected.
I now attract my soul family and like-minded kindred spirits to create a mutual
support system of fun, joy, light, and laughter.
So be it, so it is.

55: Loving · 61: Open · 97: Vulnerable

33 GUILTY

WHEN YOU FEEL guilty, it's important to examine the reason why you feel this way. I know many parents out there feel guilty if they take time for themselves. I feel instantly guilty when I see a police car, and I've never been able to figure out why. I get super paranoid that I might be doing the wrong thing or that I'm going to get into trouble somehow.

My husband, Sean, has often experienced feeling guilty from time to time, and he's pretty sure he knows where it originated. When he was about seven years old, he was accused of doing something that he didn't do. This resulted in him being taken out of elementary school and homeschooled by his mother until eighth grade. Apparently, he was accused of pooping in a urinal. Sean is very adamant to this day that it was not him.

Remember

GUILT IS CLOSELY related to remorse. If you didn't actually do something that harms another or yourself, you have nothing to feel guilty about.

If you did do something that has resulted in you feeling guilty, it is never too late to make amends for your actions. The Universe will always help you find the clarity you need to take that first step.

Dear Universe,

I now release these feelings of guilt and show up in the present moment with openness and willingness to move forward. May I seek forgiveness, self-forgiveness, and self-compassion to trust in the process as it is unfolding. ***So be it, so it is.***

35: Forgiving · 36: Free · 90: Trusting

HELPLESS

MY DAD COULD barely speak. I could tell that something was very wrong with his breathing. "I'm in the hospital; I have pneumonia."

Nothing makes you feel more helpless than when a loved one is at death's door and you're on the other side of the world. I calculated that it would take me at least 30 hours to fly to Australia from Las Vegas on such short notice. At the time, according to the nurses, he was just three hours away from being placed on life support. At 70 years old, the outlook was pretty grim.

I faced the very real possibility of not being able to say goodbye. When you feel helpless, the only thing to do is to surrender to the present moment and take one step at a time. I guided my energy toward sending my father love. In my thoughts I felt so afraid, but I kept seeing him in my mind's eye fully recovered. Thankfully, my prayers were answered, and he turned a corner! He spent an entire month in the hospital and was diagnosed with a lung disease. Miraculously, he flew to Las Vegas later that year to meet my daughter Ava for the first time. We treasured each and every moment as a celebration of the fullness of life. I now know that I will face feelings of helplessness again one day, and there is nothing I can do to avoid it.

Remember

YOU GET TO choose how you see any given situation and how you manage your energy.

You have the power to guide your emotions in each moment and celebrate the beauty and fragility of life.

Dear Universe,

I surrender this feeling of helplessness to move into a
space of trust that all is unfolding as it should.
So be it, so it is.

10: Calm · 33: Flowing · 84: Strong

35 HOPELESS

WHEN YOU FEEL hopeless, The Universe is working very fast behind the scenes to construct a solution for you. The energy of hopelessness is feeling as if all options have been exhausted, you have hit rock bottom, and there is nowhere else to go but up.

Remember

YOU WILL MOVE through this time of feeling hopeless by believing beyond what you can see. Feelings of hopelessness are often experienced in the eleventh hour before success.

The Universe can only offer solutions when you surrender to your experience. This means letting go of how you perceive your situation. You must shift your focus, tune your attention to appreciation (if you can), and remember that anything is possible if you hold faith in your heart.

Dear Universe,

Please amplify the feeling of faith and hope within my heart. Remind me that I am on a journey and this experience is all part of the divine plan.
So be it, so it is.

13: Clear · 34: Focused · 65: Positive

36 HUMILIATED

HUMILIATION AND EMBARRASSMENT are close cousins, but humiliation cuts deeper. Humiliation is traumatic and often kept quiet, whereas embarrassment, with the blessing of hindsight, can eventually be transformed into a funny story.

Since the dawn of humanity, people have intentionally humiliated others in order to gain power and prove a point — the atrocities of slavery, when Jesus was crucified, when women were hunted down and accused of witchcraft, "tarring and feathering" lawbreakers, and the unthinkable acts of humiliation leading up to the murder of six million Jews in World War II.

Placing shame and guilt on another human being will never create change or generate true power. Whatever you're going through right now, please try to place your awareness into the energy of perspective.

Remember

HUMILIATION CAN NEVER prove a point or create change. It only manifests pain.

If someone has intentionally humiliated you, you must remember your own magnificence. You are uniquely YOU. It's an invitation from The Universe to rise above the pain and heal. Another aspect is to try (if you can) to hold compassion for the people who just don't understand.

Dear Universe,

I allow this experience to flow through me and not remain in my body, mind, or spirit complex. May I hold compassion for others that are unable to see the truth. May I release the burden and the story of this feeling so that my heart feels free to move forward into a space of love.

So be it, so it is.

8: Brave · 35: Forgiving · 97: Vulnerable

(37) INDIFFERENT

JUDITH AND ROSS had been married for nearly 34 years. At the beginning of their relationship they were so in love with one another. As the years went by, they slowly drifted into their own separate corners. There was safety in the monotony of their daily lives. They didn't speak up about how they were both feeling. In fact, they didn't speak much at all.

"What's for dinner?"

"Have you taken the trash out?"

It was very a very basic level of connection. Judith would be either doing a sudoku or reading a romance novel. Ross would be watching sports on TV and drinking beer with his feet up, waiting for his dinner.

They both felt indifferent about the relationship, and they both took one another for granted. It was like they were waiting for something exciting to happen.

Remember

IF YOU FEEL indifferent about something and you don't make a decision, sometimes The Universe makes one for you. You can't sit around and wait for life to happen to you, because it's happening through you.

Ross was diagnosed with pancreatic cancer and given four months to live. Within two weeks of this sad news, Judith had a stroke and was placed on life support. Ross spent the rest of his life wishing things were different.

Dear Universe,

May I remember that life is not a dress rehearsal and that my experiences are shaped by my decisions. How I show up will be directly reflected by my sense of purpose and appreciation. Guide me, and remind me of my power.

So be it, so it is.

3: Aligned · 13: Clear · 62: Passionate

38 INSECURE

IF YOU'RE FEELING insecure, it's because you are comparing yourself to someone else.

Remember

COMPARISON IS THE thief of joy.

Or alternatively, perhaps you don't feel worthy enough. I know for myself, that if I were walking on a beach in a bikini, I would feel terrified and extremely insecure. This isn't a new development. I felt this way long before I had four children. I've always been way too much in my head about what others think of me and how they perceive me visually. This has actually warped my sense of self. It's taken a considerable amount of time for me to see the truth behind what's really going on.

I've felt insecure at 98 pounds and insecure at 200 pounds. It's a self-esteem issue.

Insecurity works in layers and levels. Even though I wouldn't feel 100 percent comfortable walking on a beach in a bikini, I would feel 100 percent confident enough to get on a stage and speak. I've also gotten to a point in my life where I realized that I have nothing to prove to anyone else. I'm not looking to gain approval. The only approval I need is from myself. Whatever body shape you have, whatever income, relationship, or any other perceived flaws or self-criticism, give yourself full permission to own your own uniqueness. This is the fastest way to rise above feeling insecure. And if you happen to see me on a beach somewhere in a bikini, feel free to give me a high five.

Dear Universe,

I am enough. I am worthy. I am perfect just the way I am right now in this moment. In times when I forget my uniqueness, send me a sign to remember my own magnificence.
So be it, so it is.

15: Confident · 36: Free · 91: Unashamed

39 IRRITATED

FEELING IRRITATED CAN be so frustrating. If you're already feeling annoyed by pretty much everything around you, then your awareness can sometimes go into sensory overdrive. Going to the movies on a Friday night to see a scary movie is usually my ultimate trigger for getting irritated. During the super scary scenes, the teenagers will scream and then laugh and then talk about it. By this stage I'm in low-grade irritability mode. Then I'll see people checking their phones, so the darkness is illuminated by tiny screens, and that's a distraction from the movie. By the time high-grade irritability kicks in, I can hear people chewing and eating popcorn, and those sounds really take me over the edge. In my mind, I'm having fantasy conversations where I'm telling everyone off like an insane headmistress of a private school.

Remember

THE KEY TO not getting irritated is to identify your triggers. Take a moment to breathe through it, and remember that the more you fuel your frustration, the more amplified it will become in your reality.

Irritation is your soul begging with you to see the irony of the situation. Babies crying on planes or in restaurants, slow service in a restaurant, waiting at the DMV, and being stuck in traffic are all great examples of sacred assignments from The Universe to cultivate presence and patience. It's easier said than done.

Dear Universe,

May I remain calm in the eye of the storm. I am willing to take a breath and not make the situation worse than it is. Allow me to release these feelings of tension in my mind and my body so that I can be fully present in this moment.
So be it, so it is.

10: Calm · 11: Cheerful · 71: Relaxed

40 JEALOUS

TARA AND JEN had been best friends since kindergarten. In their 30s, they were both single and looking for "The One" to settle down and have babies with. Dating apps, the club scene, and picking up guys at bars would never result in finding Prince Charming. Being single was the main, obsessive topic of conversation. That was until Jen manifested her soulmate in a bookstore. She met Joseph, and their whirlwind romance lead to marriage and the birth of twin baby girls — all within two years. Tara felt so jealous. In fact, her inability to not feel truly happy for Jen meant that their lifelong friendship ended abruptly.

Remember

IF YOU FEEL jealous and you can't celebrate the success of others, then you cut yourself off from the energy of your own happily ever after.

The key is to gently guide yourself to a space where you can feel happy for others who manifest what you want. Being able to genuinely wish others well is a process that takes time to master, but it's imperative that you do.

If you feel jealous, then please allow this to be your meditation:

Dear Universe,

Replace feelings of jealousy with feelings of joy for the success I am able to see. May I tune in to that energy so I can manifest on the same level. I now remember this phrase and use it accordingly: "What I wish for you, I wish for myself."
So be it, so it is.

20: Delighted · 44: Happy · 65: Positive

41 JUDGED

FEELING LIKE YOU'VE been judged unfairly is awful. Most of us just want people to like who we are and keep their negative thoughts to themselves. When you put yourself out there as a public figure, or if you sell a product online, or even if you just have an eBay account or post photos on social media, you are opening yourself up to being judged. In fact, many people hold themselves back from sharing their gifts because of the fear of being judged.

When it happens, your heart sinks, and you have a choice of how to manage your energy. You can either allow it to change who you are, or you can see it for what it is. In my work, reaching millions of people around the world, I thankfully only have a couple of "nasty" judgment-based reviews out there. At first, I felt devastated because I wanted everyone to like me. After some time, I could see that the people who would openly voice their judgments of me were in fact airing their own projections and disowned parts of themselves.

Remember

WHAT OTHERS THINK of you is none of your business.

The next time you feel as if someone has the wrong idea about you, or that you are being unfairly represented, take the time to tune in to the truth. One person's opinion does not and will never define who you are.

Dear Universe,

I send love and compassion to the people who judge me.
I refuse to hang on to the energy that does not serve me. I release my assumptions, insecurities, and concerns over to you to set free.
So be it, so it is.

42: Grounded · 69: Protected · 85: Supported

42 JUDGMENTAL

IT'S PRETTY TRICKY to catch yourself when you're in the mode of being judgmental. I remember when my next-door neighbor's husband had an affair. They had three children together, and he ended up leaving his wife for the younger woman. The news circulated throughout the community of mothers at the school.

"How could he do that? He's so despicable!"

I remember judging the situation without knowing any details and without it being any of my business. I just knew that based on my values I would never have an affair and break apart my family. At the time, I was clearly in denial about my own failing marriage and the violence that would occur at regular intervals. I demonized infidelity as the catalyst that would cause irreparable damage.

Remember

WHEN YOU JUDGE the actions of another and declare it wrong, you become the energy of what you are judging. However, what if you hold compassion? What if you could see a bigger picture at play?

For me, I ended up having an affair just months after being so judgmental of my neighbor. The Universe heard my call of judgment and sent me a mission. I was to remember that unless we walk a mile in someone else's shoes, then we have no business thinking we understand the full scope of the situation.

Dear Universe,

May I see situations which trigger judgment as an opportunity
to lean into compassion and understanding. May I see all people and
actions that cross my path through your eyes.
So be it, so it is.

 # LAZY

IF YOU'RE UNWILLING to work or use your energy, you are being lazy. My grandmother used to say that idle hands do the Devil's work. However, there are times in life when you just can't be bothered to do something. It could be that you are dragging your feet because you have to fold a giant pile of laundry. Or perhaps you have appointments to make, bills to pay, or chores to complete. My advice is that you should never put off until tomorrow what can be done today.

Remember

JUST STARTING WITH taking small steps will help you rise above the funk of laziness.

There is something magical about rolling up your sleeves to do physical work. It moves the energy and helps you to feel better emotionally. Laziness is saying to The Universe that you're not willing to play full out. You'll sit on the sidelines and happily watch as life passes you by. I know it sounds harsh, but it will hopefully motivate you to get up off your lazy butt and take action!

If you know that you're being lazy and you want to do something about it, then ask The Universe for help . . .

Dear Universe,

Present me with opportunities in my life that don't allow me to be lazy.
Release the energy of "I'll do it later" and guide me to show up in my life
with presence, persistence, and vibrant energy to get things done.
May I now manifest the essence of motivation.
So be it, so it is.

4: Aware · 19: Dedicated · 58: Motivated

 # LONELY

MY MOST MEANINGFUL "Dear Universe" moment was birthed from loneliness.

I lived in Gothenburg, Sweden, for a year in 2004. Moving from Australia to a non-English-speaking country where I didn't know anyone was pretty scary. For the first two weeks, the only people I spoke to were my husband (a man of few words) and my son, Thomas, who was three at the time. I instantly regretted the move because I missed my family and friends so much.

We didn't have the Internet connected in our apartment, so I tore out a map I found in the local phone book to take with me on walks in case I got lost. I would walk through the snow-covered cobblestoned streets hearing people converse in Swedish. I felt so lonely. I craved conversation! I realized that the only way I would cure my loneliness was to step out of my comfort zone and find new friends. I went back to the phone book in our apartment and looked up "English-speaking playgroups" for expatriate parents with toddlers. There was only one option available. It was a one-hour tram ride to a place called Frölunda — which seemed to be in the middle of nowhere. When I arrived, there were other women in similar situations with husbands who worked 60-hour weeks. I found my tribe, my new support system, and a way of easing the loneliness.

 *Remember*

YOU ARE NEVER alone. The Universe is always there to guide you to take inspired action to find new friends.

 *Dear Universe,*

Guide me to attract new friends who are fun to be around.
May we experience laughter, joy, and lightheartedness together.
So be it, so it is.

54: Loved · 85: Supported · 98: Welcomed

45 LOST

DO YOU FEEL a little lost right now? Sometimes life will take us on a magical detour into not knowing what we want or how we want to show up in the world. It might feel as if you have a tangled rainbow Slinky, and it's tremendously difficult to unravel the situation.

My career path has ventured into so many different directions over the years. One thing I know for sure is that before each transition, I had a feeling of being lost, like my train was off the tracks and I was stuck in a maze. I have started and stopped three degrees — journalism, art, and psychology. I would drift for a while trying to figure out what I wanted to "be" — I wanted to be a social media expert, an artist, a doctor, a journalist, a horror movie writer, a full-time mother. What I didn't realize at the time was that I was searching for meaning. I was searching for an identity that I could call mine.

Remember

IF YOU FEEL lost, it's just temporary. You'll find your way again. You'll feel inspired, connected, and guided in perfect divine timing.

The fastest way to snap yourself out of feeling lost is to be of service to others in need. Go to a soup kitchen and volunteer your time. Or get out a sketchbook and invent something. Write poetry. Join your local library. Whatever you do, make the gentle journey from your head into your heart. And when you find yourself in the present moment you'll remember that you can never be lost.

Dear Universe,

I am grounded in this present moment. I remember that I am on a spiritual journey. I honor the process of feeling lost in order to find passion and purpose within the stillness.
So be it, so it is.

13: Clear · 51: Inspired · 89: Transformative

 # 46 MAD

MY DAD WOULD always tell the story of his aunt Polly. I don't even know if this really happened.

Polly and Jack had a son who was about five years old. He was just small enough to place in a bucket and send down their well (on the farm) to see if there was a blockage in the pump. Polly pleaded with Jack not to lower the boy down into the darkness. She felt intuitively that something could go horribly wrong. There must have been a gas leak or toxic fumes, because when they retrieved the bucket, the boy was lifeless.

Polly and Jack's relationship was never the same. Jack would sit down to eat his breakfast, and find a note Polly left on his plate saying: "You did it, Jack."

Her madness manifested in obsessively writing those four words everywhere she could.

"You did it, Jack."

On the walls, the mirrors, the furniture. Polly was so mad at Jack that she became mentally ill and had to be institutionalized for the rest of her life.

Now, this is an extreme case of how feeling mad can drive you to madness. This is why it's so important to not get mad at the small stuff. Feeling angry, irritated, or impatient with others is The Universe asking you to rise above it. For Aunt Polly, her heart never healed because the madness consumed her.

Remember

YOU CAN CHOOSE how you respond to situations. Life will be full of things that make you mad. Your job is to make sure that it doesn't consume you.

Dear Universe,

May I now release all feelings of anger and of being mad.
May I be returned to my natural state of peace, joy, love, and happiness.
So be it, so it is.

10: Calm · 35: Forgiving · 86: Surrendered

47 MANIC

IN PSYCHOLOGY, MANIC refers to a state of heightened activity and emotions. There are many frenzied characteristics of a manic episode. When one unfolds, it can fall under the umbrella of mental illness, drug use, or even elevated levels of stress. If you're going through this, please know that you are not alone, and you will be okay.

It was early 2009. I was the only member of my family who had a car. The appointment for the rehab clinic was for 8 a.m. I would collect my sister from my father's house, because she had finally agreed to book herself in for treatment. My daughter Olivia was about three years old, and I had to bring her with me.

We arrived at my dad's house to find him sitting on top of my sister, holding her down because she was threatening to stab him with a carving knife. He pinned her wrist to the floor because she was about to wield the blade. As soon as Olivia and I walked in, they pretended like nothing was happening, despite the fact they were still in a weird position on the floor.

"Is that chocolate, Granddad?" asked Olivia.

"Yes, my darling. Help yourself."

Olivia grabbed the bag of chocolates and sat outside on the porch to eat them. This helped to provide a distraction from the situation.

My sister was manic in this moment. It was scary. She would either wish to inflict harm on others, or on herself. That afternoon she was admitted to a psychiatric ward only to escape, return home, and pretend like nothing ever happened.

The state of being manic is when you are abnormally heightened in your response to people and experiences. Many sensitive souls tend to have manic episodes.

Remember

IF YOU EVER feel like you are being manic, please seek help and support immediately. There are people who can help you move through your experience.

If a manic episode isn't your first rodeo, tune in to the energy of The Universe for guidance during this time . . .

Dear Universe,

Allow me to take a deep breath and hold it. As I exhale, may I now release the tension and energy that is moving through this moment. Give me the strength to pause, stop, and seek support. I am loved, all is well.
So be it, so it is.

5: Balanced · 63: Peaceful · 85: Supported

(48) MANIPULATIVE

I'D LIKE TO congratulate you! If you can identify that you are feeling manipulative, you are about to create a powerful transformation in your awareness. The essence and energy behind acts of manipulation are unfair and unkind.

Remember

THE ENERGY YOU put out there will always return to you.

Take April, for example. She was in her late 30s and desperately wanted to have a baby. Her biological clock was ticking so loudly that she didn't care who the father was — only that she create a baby before her time ran out.

April quite frequently attended business conferences for the company she worked for. During the evenings there were networking events at the bar. Tequila flowed freely, and as a single gal she quite often hooked up with one of the gentlemen. April kept a small assortment of condoms in her purse. Before each event she carefully poked tiny holes through the packets in the hope that she would get pregnant.

April's intention was not only dangerous, but manipulative. There's an investment banker out there somewhere in the world who doesn't know that he has seven-year-old twin boys — both with severe learning disabilities and extremely high medical bills for a single mother to pay with her welfare check.

If you are feeling like taking manipulative action, show yourself some compassion and ask The Universe to redirect your energy and choose a better path:

Dear Universe,

I am honest and open. I make decisions based on integrity and I am aware of the impact that my decisions and actions have on others. May I forgive myself and my past and release my need to control others.

So be it, so it is.

20: Delighted · 25: Empowered · 61: Open

49 MISUNDERSTOOD

ONE OF THE toughest emotional experiences is being misunderstood by other people. It can cause a great deal of pain when you see, hear, or witness someone expressing a false perception of who you are.

The rise of feeling misunderstood has escalated since the birth of social media. Online bullying and cyberstalking are very real elements to consider. Teenagers have committed suicide from the horrendous pressure of online trolls. As a person who has a very visible online presence, I have experienced my fair share of nasty comments, assumptions, and judgments.

Remember

OTHER PEOPLE CAN'T mess with your energy. You know who you are and where your heart is.

There is a natural tendency to try and prove yourself or gain the approval of others when you feel misunderstood. This is pointless. You're wasting your energy.

When you remember that what other people think of you is none of your business, then life is sweeter for you. My meditation teacher used to say: "Criticize me all you want, take my karma."

I'm not sure how that works exactly, but what I do know is that the energy that you put out there will return to you.

When you feel like the real you isn't being seen, ask The Universe to remind you of your truth . . .

Dear Universe,

I ask that I may release the unfair assumptions and judgments of others. I know where my heart is; I live my life in truth and integrity. I now send out the energy of resolution to this situation so that I am allowed the space to feel heard.
So be it, so it is.

2: Adored · 77: Seen · 85: Supported

50 MOODY

THE SOUND OF your spouse chewing food seems to be five times louder and annoying than it usually is. Your kids are normally well behaved, but they might be really bugging you to the point that you need to hide in the closet and eat ice cream in solitude. You might even find yourself snapping at people or not being aware of your tone of voice. These are true stories, by the way! I have ridden the pesky wave of moodiness for many years.

Moodiness can strike when you least want it, or expect it. It's the perfect storm for even the shortest of fuses to ignite and explode.

Whether you're hormonal, tired, triggered, or hangry (angry because you're hungry), there are things you can do in order to guide your emotional volatility to a better space.

Remember

YOU GET TO identify when you need to shift your mood. If you're content being in a sullen state, gently allow it to move through your experience as long as you don't upset people in the process.

Mood swings are the worst for your loved ones. Be mindful of this. Try and use visualization techniques and affirm that you are cool, calm, and collected.

Dear Universe,

I ask that I flow with the energy of being centered and still from within. May I release the need to control the circumstances and people around me. Show me ways that I can be nonreactive, present, and grateful for this moment.
So be it, so it is.

5: Balanced · 71: Relaxed · 83: Still

51 MORTIFIED

HAVE YOU EVER had one of those dreams where you are naked in a public place or perhaps there are no doors in the restroom and you're on the toilet? I feel like this is the true essence of mortification — when your "privates" become public.

I can't believe I'm about to share this story, but for the sake of illustrating how to move through the feeling, I am willing to take one for the team!

Let's just say my situation involved being 15 years old, on a school excursion to the Melbourne Zoo, with a boy I liked, when I had my period, and I was wearing white pants! I think that paints an adequate picture of how that scenario went horribly wrong. Thankfully, my friend had a sweater to lend me that I could tie around my waist to hide the bright-red catastrophe from behind.

Remember

WHEN YOU FEEL mortified or embarrassed by something, it's okay to laugh. Humor always helps to move you through a situation with ease and grace.

Whether your parents walk in on you and your partner when you're having sex, you vomit in a public place, or you step in dog poop and accidentally walk it through a fancy interior design store, just know that The Universe is all about divine comedy.

Dear Universe,

Help me to move through this feeling of mortification right now.
Help me to laugh at this situation and remember that it will one day make a really funny story to share with my friends. I'll be okay.
So be it, so it is.

11: Cheerful · 15: Confident · 91: Unashamed

52 NEGATIVE

IF YOU CAN identify that you're being negative, then congratulations! I'd say that the vast majority of humans out there cannot see when they are perpetually stuck on the mode of looking for things that aren't right in life. Is your glass half empty, or half full?

When you constantly look for things to be negative about, to complain about, or to criticize, you are pinching yourself off from the flow of The Universe. Good things cannot be attracted to you in this state.

Remember

DON'T BE AFRAID of feeling negative. Allow it to be and flow through your experience. Bad days are designed to make the good days even sweeter and more meaningful.

You see, darkness has to coexist with lightness. It's a constant dance. The difference is in your awareness of when it attaches itself to your reality. If you're regularly saying things like "nothing good ever happens to me," then ask yourself how you can contribute to making your day uplifting and inspiring. You can climb out of a negative rut by looking for things to be grateful for.

And if all else fails, then do a meditation with The Universe to ask the grumpiness to leave the building . . .

Dear Universe,

There is so much in life to feel grateful for. There is so much in life to feel happy about. When I have my moments of negativity, sadness, or frustration, may I remember that it's an opportunity to rise above it.
So be it, so it is.

4: Aware · 41: Grateful · 44: Happy

53 NUMB

I KEPT A bottle of cherry vodka hidden in the linen closet next to the bedroom. In the evenings before bed, I would secretly take three swigs. It was just enough to numb myself from the monotony of having sex with my then-husband, Max. I didn't want to feel anything because I knew that I was never being truly seen or valued. Or at least, I never allowed myself to be seen because of the emotional pain I was in. During the act, I felt like I wasn't there. I definitely wasn't in the mood to be intimate most of the time, because of how upset I felt in my heart. Max and I were so disconnected from one another, it wasn't fair to either one of us. When this cycle is created within a relationship, it can be like a thick fog that never lifts until you become aware that you have the power to create change.

Remember

WHEN YOU FEEL numb, you disassociate and disconnect yourself from the present moment and the flow of The Universe.

If you feel like this, The Universe is pleading with you to wake up and smell the roses. There is so much beauty and wonder in this world we live in. We get to choose how we show up in each moment — and if we can't, we need to dismantle the reality and choose again.

Whatever you do, please don't choose self-destructive behavior to make yourself feel. Self-harm is not a solution to drawing out your emotions. As a sentient being, you deserve to feel. You must feel in order to live a healthy life. How we feel is what constructs the fabric of our reality. Numbness is a symptom of unplugging from Oneness. If this sounds like you, please be gentle with yourself. Also, use this feeling as a prompt to choose a different path for yourself if you can.

To begin moving out of numbness, make a list of things you can do today that are the most self-loving and then declare this statement to The Universe:

Dear Universe,

May I allow myself to feel the power and the beauty of
the present moment. I now remove myself from situations, people, and places
that don't spark the magnificence of life force within me. May my emotions
find the sacred space they need to be authentically expressed.
So be it, so it is.

3: Aligned · 26: Energized · 85: Supported

 OBSESSIVE

IF YOU ARE currently obsessing over something or someone, this is a gentle reminder to shift your focus.

Remember

YOUR ROLE IS to trust that The Universe will deliver your desires in perfect divine timing.

A key phrase to remember when you're fixated on a certain outcome is to affirm: "This or something better."

Take Nate, for example. He was romantically interested in this guy at work named Avi. Avi was newly single, and Nate was eagerly awaiting the opportunity to ask him out on a date, since they obviously had some chemistry going on. So one Friday afternoon, Nate finally sent him a text and patiently waited for a reply. He waited and waited and obsessively checked his phone almost every 30 seconds. As the old saying goes: "A watched pot never boils."

The obsession turned into self-doubt, fear, and concern that perhaps he was being rejected. By Sunday night, he still hadn't heard a thing from Avi. He decided to go out to dinner with some friends to take his mind off the pain of waiting. Nate had a few drinks and then went dancing with his friend Stacy. They danced for over an hour. Nate was out of his head and into his heart on the dance floor. Can you guess what happened next? He received a text from Avi saying that he'd love to go on a date very soon.

The Universe is awesome when we move (or dance) ourselves out of our own way.

Dear Universe,

I am now ready to release the energy of my desired outcome.
May obsession be replaced with trust and faith that the perfect situation will appear exactly as it should. I implicitly trust in the process.
So be it, so it is.

48: Hopeful · 61: Open · 86: Surrendered

55 OVERWHELMED

WHEN YOU FEEL overwhelmed, it is literally like having too many tabs open on your computer, and all you see is the tiny rainbow spinning wheel. When you're in overwhelm mode, your system is likely headed for a crash. It's like the circus performer juggling too many things at once. The truth? It's just not a sustainable place to remain, so you have to peel things back to a basic level.

Remember

ALL THAT EXISTS is the present moment, the now.

If you have too many items on your to-do list, constant requests from your family, bills to pay, and an endless agenda of tasks to complete . . . then STOP. Remember that unless you look after yourself first, you won't be able to get anything completed in the long run.

I've been in overwhelm mode many times in my life. Now I turn my attention inward and ask myself what I need in order to slow down and take a moment to remember my point of power. Make a cup of tea, take a walk or a nap, run yourself a nice bath — whatever it takes to slow down and not allow the energy of frantic expectation to consume you.

Dear Universe,

I now breathe in the energy of serenity. I exhale feelings of stress
and overwhelm. May I hold the awareness that time is fleeting and the urgency
of physical tasks is an illusion that I will tend to when I feel a little stronger.
So be it, so it is.

5: Balanced · 36: Free · 80: Serene

56 OVERWORKED

ARE YOU FEELING overworked right now? If you are, it's time to allow yourself to get some rest and regenerate. If you're feeling irritated or annoyed by the work you do, perhaps it's time to put things into perspective.

Remember

THE ENERGY YOU bring to your job will either energize you or drain you. The choice is yours.

Working and being of service to others is the lifeblood of humanity. Everyone plays a vital role on this stage called "life." Whether you're doing what you love or just working a job to pay the bills, remember that being aware of your energy will either contribute to your life or contaminate it.

Feeling overworked is a call from The Universe to seek more time to play and to be joyful in the present moment. I love seeing people who have extremely difficult, boring, or physically demanding jobs bring so much joy to their experience. Gardeners, house cleaners, childcare workers, teachers, nurses, DMV clerks, postal workers, bank tellers . . . and the list goes on! These are the true angels in life — they show up and serve, even if they feel overworked.

Connect to The Universe to spark the process of energizing your perspective . . .

Dear Universe,

I am now ready to recharge so that I can show up for my work with the energy of enthusiasm, service, and gratitude.
So be it, so it is.

46: Helpful · 73: Rested · 90: Trusting

57 PAINED

DIFFERENT PEOPLE HAVE different pain thresholds. One person might give birth effortlessly, where another person might have a near-death experience because she feels like she is pushing a watermelon through the eye of a needle! If you feel pained on a regular basis — whether it's physical pain or emotional pain — please know that there are several ways you can ease your discomfort, such as alternative therapies and meditation.

When Sean randomly got his little toe caught in a laundry basket, he swore it was the worst pain he had ever felt in his life. For me, it was when the epidural and anesthetic wore off during my C-section giving birth to my daughter Lulu. To each their own!

Remember

YOU ARE A spiritual being. The pain only exists in the physical realm. Allow your awareness to call upon the nonphysical strength when you need it.

This is why hypnosis and alternative therapies such as EFT (emotional freedom technique) and reiki (energetic healing) can be so powerful.

The next time you feel pained, or if you are presently in pain, please ask The Universe for assistance . . .

Dear Universe,

I now release this pain from my body, my mind, and my spirit. May it be replaced with strength to heal. May my being be infused with light, love, and courage.
So be it, so it is.

3: Aligned · 44: Happy · 45: Healed

58 PANICKED

OVER THE YEARS, my mother would tell the story of my birth. She went into labor on the night of Halloween. The next day, in the first moments of my grand entrance into the world, I panicked. The umbilical cord slipped over my head. As my mother pushed, I was being strangled. My first experience was probably a near-death experience. Apparently, when I was finally out, I was blue. There was a deafening silence in the room. Everyone (including me) was holding their breath! As my mother's third child, and the first one she could keep, my birth created panic from my own panic. After a few whacks on the back, I cried!

My mother would always call me a "Panicky Percy" — meaning that panic is my expected mode when I get stressed. Luckily I feel I've released that pattern because of cultivating the awareness that it "strangles" my energy.

Remember

PANIC IS AN opportunity to slow down and go with the flow.

Breathing slowly can be a great method to navigate panic. If a situation or person demands your immediate and urgent attention, remember that you can guide your energy internally to a space of stillness. Use this as your anchor point to the present moment . . .

Dear Universe,

I am grounded in the present moment. May I breathe in the energy of presence,
may I exhale the frantic energy of panic. All is well, I am safe, I am loved.
So be it, so it is.

5: Balanced · 69: Protected · 71: Relaxed

59 PARANOID

PARANOIA IS THE extreme feeling of being fearful. To consciously see it in action and recognize it is a true gift. Once the seeds of paranoia are planted, it's a slippery slope to return from. The good news is that you can, if you are willing to take a peek beyond the illusion of being afraid of worst-case scenarios.

Remember

BEING FEARFUL OF the future is your call from The Universe to build trust and to see your situation clearly.

You can be paranoid for the smallest of reasons, such as being afraid you have lipstick on your teeth, that your child is going to choke and die, that a giant tsunami might destroy the world — the list could potentially be infinite.

Your role is to remember that you have a choice in how to guide your energy. For instance, there are so many versions of the Chicken Little fable. In one version, he was so distressed that the "sky was falling" when an acorn fell on his head, that he drew the paranoid conclusion that his life would end soon and went into a mad panic. The moral of the story is that courage is imperative and that when we make a bigger deal of things than they are, then life gets crazy. We've all done it. We've all blown things out of proportion or been suspicious about things or people or events that are yet to unfold. Paranoia will always lead you down a path that spirals. However, when you consciously stop it from progressing, then you win.

Dear Universe,

Allow me to see the truth in my present situation and not make it worse than it is. May I release the feelings of paranoia and swap them for trust that your wisdom and guidance is supporting me on my journey.
So be it, so it is.

10: Calm · 75: Safe · 90: Trusting

60 PERSECUTED

IF YOU FEEL persecuted for your beliefs, your sexuality, your race, your gender, or causes you feel passionate about, then remember that you never have to explain yourself to someone else. We must lead with love and lead by example.

This should be a deal breaker in relationships, both personal and professional. Yes, we know that the fine art of conversation means avoiding the themes of politics or religion — however, if you feel the need to say sorry for what you believe in, no matter what it is, you're moving in the wrong circles. You have 100 percent permission to believe in whatever you wish as long as you don't intentionally hurt people in order to prove a point.

Remember

YOUR BELIEFS ARE your own and the compass for your soul. Stand strong in the energy of what you feel passionate about, how you can voice the need for change, and what you can do to draw healthy boundaries.

The root energy of people who persecute others is ignorance. If you can, hold compassion for people who welcome conflict and discord into their lives willingly. Also be aware that a majority of people have blind spots where they are totally unaware of their own behavior, how their biases manifest, and that there are ways to have meaningful conversations without judgment or violence.

Dear Universe,

Remind me that I am who I am. May I proudly maintain my
energy and beliefs with an open heart. Allow me to hold compassion
for people who have forgotten that we are all part of the
same beautiful fabric of Oneness.
So be it, so it is.

8: Brave · 25: Empowered · 36: Free

⑥ PESSIMISTIC

DO YOU TEND to see the worst aspect of things or believe that the worst will happen? If you're feeling pessimistic, it's because life has probably treated you unfairly in the past. You've probably had your heart broken or your dreams shattered, or you've surrounded yourself with a whole bunch of party poopers. It's okay. It's normal. But what's great about this is the realization and awareness that you can choose a different path for yourself.

Remember

IF YOU CHANGE your feelings and thoughts, you watch the world around you radically change.

Feeling pessimistic is an opportunity presented to you by The Universe to open your heart to limitless possibilities. A more gentle approach that could help you might be to expect the best and prepare for the worst. This simple flip in your awareness could change the way you brace yourself for the experiences you have throughout life.

Life is not meant to be difficult and full of obstacles. That's all external. It's your internal way of managing and perceiving any obstacles as they arise that will determine if you are successful or not.

Dear Universe,

May I now release my old pattern of expecting the worst
before it happens. May I remember that my energy today is paving
the way for my experience of tomorrow.
So be it, so it is.

33: Flowing · 65: Positive · 85: Supported

62 POWERLESS

> "When we are no longer able to change
> a situation, we are challenged to change ourselves."
> — VIKTOR E. FRANKL

MANY PEOPLE EXPERIENCE feeling powerless, which can sometimes be the theme for a lifetime. If you feel powerless, The Universe wants you to remember your power. You are so powerful. All you have to do is take a peek into your past to see where you handed your power over and to whom. Spend some time with your journal, writing out possible experiences or seasons in your life where you felt like you had no control or no voice, or felt invisible.

Remember

YOU CAN CLAIM your power and access it whenever you need it. You just have to trust that it's there, always.

Many children feel powerless when they hear their parents argue. When you experience health issues, you might feel powerless. Or when life isn't delivering enough money to cover your lifestyle expenses, then powerlessness can rear its ugly head. The key piece of information to imprint into your subconscious mind is to own your power.

You are a continuation of the almighty energetic flow of The Universe. It's flowing through you! It's as if you are a superhero and you have forgotten your powers. Life can only show up and create new and exciting experiences for you if you can step into your power enough to receive the gifts. Let go of the old version of you. Shed your skin like a snake and visualize what your superhero costume would look like. Do you have a cape? A color scheme? A crown? A magical ability? Visualize this character within you, helping you to build the courage to overcome any of the times you feel powerless.

Dear Universe,

I am powerful. I am strong. I am brave. I am extremely grateful for the opportunity to show up in life with my core strengths and superpowers. I have let go of my past and I am compassionate, fierce, and empowered in the present.
So be it, so it is.

25: Empowered · 66: Powerful · 84: Strong

63 REPRESSED

EVER TRIED TO hold a beach ball underwater? You can't for too long. There's a lot of resistance. This also happens when you try to hide or disown who you really are. Repression can happen in the most unlikely ways. It can occur with people who try to deny their true sexuality or gender. It can even happen when people push their feelings to the side and don't allow themselves to feel the fullness and wholeness of the beautiful human condition.

Remember

YOU ARE ALLOWED to be and express yourself in any way that you wish or desire. This is your life.

Violet was married several times before she had the thought that perhaps she liked women. There had always been a natural attraction, but she never stopped to fully examine if she would ever think of being in a relationship with someone of the same gender. Born in the 1920s, in England, meant that she was forced into a lifestyle of societal conformity based on the expectations of others. Even after being married three times Violet knew that there had to be more meaning and connection in a relationship.

Violet didn't meet Rhonda until she was in her sixties. Rhonda had lived the "lifestyle" for her entire life and Violet didn't feel as if she was truly living until they joined their lives together in union.

If you feel as if you are not able to express the real you to the world, remember that The Universe adores you and loves you unconditionally.

Dear Universe,

I ask for support to build the courage to express my feelings from a space of authenticity. I ask that you guide me through this process and attract the right people to advocate for me at this time.

So be it, so it is.

47: Honest · 85: Supported · 91: Unashamed

 **RESENTFUL**

IF YOU FEEL resentment toward someone, it's toxic for your own well-being. The energy behind resentment is comprised of the three basic emotions of disgust, sadness, and surprise — the perception of the event of injustice. When you feel this way, it becomes incredibly difficult to return. The Universe presents you with one of the most challenging situations to rise above.

Once you harbor that energy in your heart, forgiveness is the only way to overcome the damage. However, it takes a brave and kind soul to venture into this profoundly spiritual work.

There have been people in my life who I have resented, even hated. I don't make that statement lightly. Whether it's a coworker or a friend, it's easy to draw a deep line in the sand and set a boundary. When it's your spouse or a member of your family, overcoming resentment becomes a sacred spiritual mission. It can either be a success or a failure — there is no middle ground.

Resentment is like grief; it changes who you are.

Remember

WHEN YOU ARE willing to release the resentment and bitterness, The Universe will reward you for your bravery.

There are infinite rewards in forgiveness and creating a new path for yourself. You are stronger because of the experience.

Call forth the help from The Universe to recalibrate your heart and the vibrancy of your soul . . .

Dear Universe,

Give me the strength to forgive. Release feelings of resentment.
May I draw boundaries that serve me and trust that there are divine
lessons unfolding in this experience.
So be it, so it is.

3: Aligned · 14: Compassionate · 35: Forgiving

65 RIGID

IF YOU CAN identify that you're being rigid, or alternatively, if you believe that someone else is being rigid with their beliefs or behavior, then this story will help you to gain a little perspective and insight. When I was 19, my boy-friend and I had been together for nearly two years. I lived in a tiny bungalow at the back of my parents' house. Tim would live with me for a few days a week, and we were the best of friends. However, we used to get into heated debates about the existence of God and The Universe. He said that he believed in "Isness," and that everything "is" as it should be. Furthermore, he called himself an atheist. I would literally cry myself to sleep, wishing that he believed in a higher power. Tim appeared to be so rigid with his beliefs. There was no way I was ever going to change his mind; it was made up that there was no heaven, no hell, and no cosmic force orchestrating the fabric of reality.

By me not being open to accepting his perspective and the right to have his own beliefs, I was the rigid one.

Remember

WHEN YOU CAN try and understand the perspective from someone else's point of view, you activate the magic of compassion.

Being rigid is about not allowing the flow of infinite possibilities to manifest into your reality. If you need a little help to open up to the perspective of others, ask The Universe to turn your energy back through the lens of Oneness:

Dear Universe,

I live in a unified paradigm of love, compassion, and openness. If someone doesn't hold the same perspective as I do, I send them love and I graciously agree to disagree.
So be it, so it is.

14: Compassionate · 33: Flowing · 61: Open

 **SAD**

THE DAY AFTER I lost my first pregnancy at 16 weeks, I was told to wait in the preoperative area where I noticed there were about seven or so other young women, also in white gowns, seated and waiting anxiously. The girl next to me was crying and trying to hide it.

"How do you know this is the right thing to do?" she whispered to me.

I didn't have a clue what she meant until it dawned on me that all of these women were there for abortions. I was in a public hospital, without medical insurance, sitting with a group of young women scheduled for pregnancy terminations. I didn't realize that the D&C operation after a miscarriage is pretty much the same procedure for an abortion.

I responded to the girl, gently: "I had a miscarriage."

She then went on to tell me that her mother was making her have the abortion because she still hadn't finished high school. I could feel the inner conflict within the girl, and a deep sadness. I could feel that she was torn between wanting to honor the life she was carrying, and honoring her own life in order to move forward.

It must be unimaginably hard to make that choice, and I promise you, I don't judge. It's not my place. What I do know is that the process surrounding a new life growing or not growing can create sadness.

As humans, we experience sadness for so many different reasons. Your goldfish could die, you might have your favorite TV show canceled, or someone might have eaten the last of the ice cream in the freezer. Sadness is our soul's way of showing up the contrast of life.

Remember

IF YOU FEEL sad, cry it out. Process it in your own time, in your own way. Too many people feel like they don't have the space to feel the way they want to feel. Allow yourself the room for sadness, so it can be processed faster.

The Universe is always supporting you through this process . . .

Dear Universe,

May I move from the energy of sadness into hopefulness and gratitude. May I be given the perspective that this time in my life is just temporary. I trust in the journey that my heart is being healed as it is meant to.
So be it, so it is.

16: Connected · 41: Grateful · 48: Hopeful

67 SCARED

IF YOU FEEL scared right now, your number 1 priority is to make yourself feel safe. There are so many reasons that you might feel this way at this time. Perhaps you are waiting for some news, an outcome, or a diagnosis. Perhaps your relationship is a bit rocky, and you feel afraid for what the future holds. Maybe you had a nightmare, and you're finding it difficult to get back to sleep.

Remember

BEING SCARED IS based on fear, and when you flip your awareness to surrendering and trusting that everything will work out perfectly, then you dismantle the illusion.

When I was a kid, I would sleep with my arms tucked into the bed because I thought that if I let my arm dangle over the side then a crocodile would bite it off. As a teenager, I was scared of having sex for the first time. I'd heard it was mildly unpleasant, and so I was fearful. I was scared of getting pregnant and then losing the pregnancy. You see, most of the time you're scared of things that haven't happened yet. And when you don't rise above the fear, then you are letting The Universe know that you have created space in your life for the worst-case scenario.

What if you prepared your thoughts to rise above the fear and being scared? What if the uncertainty of the future or even the present didn't have to be so darn scary? The Universe wants you to trust in the process of your life story unfolding and being written . . .

Dear Universe,

I release the feeling of being scared and replace it with unwavering faith and trust in the process of my life being lived to the fullest. I set the powerful intention to take one moment at a time and treasure it as the gift of conscious awareness. **So be it, so it is.**

8: Brave · 67: Present · 90: Trusting

68 SELFISH

SOMETIMES IT'S PERFECTLY okay to be selfish, especially when it comes to self-care — just as long as you're not compromising the well-being of others around you.

The week after my son, Thomas, was born, Max lost his job. With a newborn baby, we were forced to move back in with my parents. Since I was still a New Zealand citizen and Max was from England, we were unable to receive welfare support from the Australian government. We had no savings and no way to pay for our expenses. When Thomas was about eight weeks old, we had less than $300 to last for a few weeks. My parents were able to provide food and a roof over our heads, but we had to cover the cost of formula and diapers.

One afternoon, Max returned home with over $100 of car design magazines that he said he needed as "inspiration." I went nuts! I felt like this was the most selfish, self-centered thing to do because he was a 33-year-old man being supported by my parents! With that being said, there have been many blind spots in my own actions throughout life that have been shamefully selfish as well.

Remember

YOU MUST TAKE your actions from a space of consciousness and consideration of how those actions impact others.

If you are aware of being selfish, flip your inner switch to being of service.

Dear Universe,

May I recognize when I am being selfish instead of self-loving and aware.
May I always remember to think about how my actions will impact others.
Show me how I can be of service.
So be it, so it is.

4: Aware · 40: Gracious · 87: Thoughtful

69 SHOCKED

THE IMPACT THAT shock has on your emotional well-being can manifest in a full spectrum of different ways.

Remember

STAY CALM AND be gentle with yourself. Your central nervous system needs all the nurturing care you can muster during this time.

One of my first experiences with shock arrived on a Saturday morning when I was just 16 years old. My parents sat my sister and me down for a "little chat."

"Is Mom pregnant? Are you getting divorced? Are we moving?"

I had always thought that I was the first child my mother gave birth to when she was 25. This was not the truth — to my utter surprise! It turns out that I had two older half-brothers who my mother had given up for adoption, and she was in the process of reconnecting with and finding them. For my entire life my parents tried to protect me by keeping this huge secret. I felt lied to, I felt powerless. I was in shock. My whole world changed after one conversation.

Shock, over time, moves into a phase of acceptance of what is. It's a series of powerful steps that allow you to move through life-changing news with an open mind.

Try this meditation if you are feeling shocked by news you might have just discovered or received, or if you are in shock from a frightening experience:

Dear Universe,

I trust that my initial reaction will transform into faith very soon and I will be returned to a state of well-being. Thank you for your support, your unconditional love, and your presence in my life during this time of need.

So be it, so it is.

10: Calm · 75: Safe · 90: Trusting

 # SHY

IF YOU'RE THE quiet type, you're probably all too familiar with the scary situation of speaking in front of a group of people. The good news is that being shy isn't something you need to overcome — you just need to embrace it. There are quiet leaders in the world, shy people who have achieved amazing things and accomplished greatness. There is nothing wrong with being shy.

If you've ever been told to speak up, or to be more confident, the thing to remember is that you are uniquely you! You don't have to prove yourself to anyone, and you don't have anything to be afraid of. I might be a little shy when you first meet me, but I soon warm up.

Remember

WORK THE AWARENESS of being shy to your advantage. You don't have to be like everyone else.

Some of the world's most brilliant people are introverted by nature.

Also remember that The Universe is always with you, flowing through you when you need a healthy dose of confidence to just be yourself.

 *Dear Universe,*

May I now embrace who I am and cease to think I should be somebody else. I now appreciate my own inner strength and trust it is always expressed in my own authentic way.
So be it, so it is.

5: Balanced · 15: Confident · 96: Visible

 **SICK**

YOU MIGHT HAVE the flu, a cold, a stomach bug, or food poisoning. You might even be experiencing some kind of illness that is moving through your body as you are on the journey to being healed.

Being sick is a great opportunity to manifest wellness. In fact, as humans, it's important to remember that each day 50 to 70 billion of our cells die and are regenerated. This means we are constantly becoming new versions of ourselves.

When you get sick, it sucks. I've been pregnant ten times, so I've experienced a lot of morning sickness over the years. When I was pregnant with my daughter Lulu, I was sick for three months straight. I was able to puke neatly into my purse (lined with a trash bag of course) if I was out and about. I'd almost refined the process into an art form! When the malaise finally lifted, I felt like a brand-new person with a newfound sense of energy and purpose.

Remember

WHEN YOU ARE unwell your body is doing everything it can to seek wellness. Your job is to trust the process and remember that sickness is not going to be with you forever.

When you feel sick, connect to The Universe to accelerate your healing process . . .

Dear Universe,

I trust that you are infusing my being with the energy of wellness.
I now see myself whole, healed, and vibrant. May my immune system be strengthened and my body energized with possibility.
So be it, so it is.

45: Healed · 95: Vibrant · 99: Whole

72 STRESSED

HARVARD RESEARCHERS ESTIMATE that 80 percent of doctors' visits are caused by stress. It's also estimated that more than one in five American adults took medications for psychiatric disorders such as anxiety and depression in 2010. Stress is a silent killer, and this is why it's so important to create regular self-care rituals in order to calm down, chill out, and remember that we have the power to guide our emotions.

Remember

WHEN YOU FEEL stressed, it's a reminder that if you change your thoughts, you change your reality.

On a physical level, stress in your body will result in illness because you're producing a hormone called cortisol. This leads to weight gain, poor sleep, low sex drive, and the list goes on of things that you probably don't want to manifest. A gentle approach to guiding your thoughts and emotions is the best solution. Make the journey out of your head and into your heart. Make yourself a cup of holy basil (tulsi) tea, which contains herbal adaptogens to relieve stress, and set aside time daily to meditate and connect with The Universe.

Dear Universe,

I now release this energy of stress and replace it with self-compassion and trust that everything is taken care of in my life. I am now grounded in my heart space and reminded of the importance of self-care each and every day.
So be it, so it is.

14: Compassionate · 17: Content · 71: Relaxed

 STUCK

FEELING STUCK RIGHT now? For some people, it can feel like the movie *Groundhog Day*, where the monotony of life is amplified. You might have tried to create change or transformation, and yet nothing is moving in the direction you'd like it to. The good news about feeling stuck is that there are two components that will disrupt your reality and prompt the change and inspiration you desire. The change resides in shifting the pattern within your thoughts and words.

If you keep thinking that you're stuck, The Universe will respond with more feelings of "stuckness." If you perpetually complain about your life verbally, The Universe will deliver more of the same.

Remember

IF YOU MAKE tiny shifts in the way that you think and the words that you speak, your reality will shift almost instantly.

When you feel stuck, see it as a gift to pause and ask yourself what it is that you really want.

Dear Universe,

I ask for new, fun, and vibrant energy to manifest into my current reality. I am grateful for this time of reflection, to gain clarity and to build momentum for a new and exciting chapter in my life. All is unfolding in perfect divine timing.
So be it, so it is.

42: Grounded · 45: Healed · 89: Transformative

74 SUFFOCATED

PATTY AND JIM had been married for over 40 years. Patty chose all of the clothes for Jim to wear each day, what and when he ate, and when he slept. In social situations, Patty would even answer the questions that were asked directly to him by others. There was no space for Jim to express himself because Patty was always telling him what to do and when to do it. He felt suffocated, even though he dearly loved his wife.

Feeling like you don't have the space you need to process your emotions can lead you to feel suffocated. If someone is micromanaging you or being controlling or dominant, it can be a great cause for concern. It might feel like the collar of your shirt is too tight or that you have a plastic bag over your head (in more extreme cases).

If this sounds like you, then you are being strongly advised by The Universe to set some healthy boundaries and choose a different way to respond to your current situation.

Remember

PEOPLE WILL TREAT you in the way that you allow them to treat you. If you need space, ask for space.

Be clear with your concerns and expect that the request for space be honored.

Dear Universe,

May I now set healthy boundaries and express myself clearly so that my desire for space is honored. I hold trust that my intention is not met with resistance. May I lead with compassion and love.
So be it, so it is.

14: Compassionate · 36: Free · 71: Relaxed

75 SUICIDAL

FEELING SUICIDAL IS a very real, complicated, and frightening situation. If you feel like this right now, please reach out to someone for help immediately. There are trained people available on the phone or on a web chat to help you in your times of need. They are ready to listen compassionately and support you through this crisis: 800-273-8255 or suicidepreventionlifeline.org.

If you are reflecting on times in your life when you may have felt suicidal, please know that you are not alone.

Remember

LIFE IS PRECIOUS. There may be times in your life that you feel like you're never going to be okay, but you will get through this!

Our lives have seasons. You will have good days, and you will have bad days, and it's all perfectly normal and part of the plan. Please remember that there is no shame in asking for support.

Dear Universe,

I have officially hit rock bottom, and the only way is up. I am open to allowing others to support and guide me back to a place of emotional well-being. This season of my life will pass. I am going to be okay.

So be it, so it is.

84: Strong · 85: Supported · 90: Trusting

76 SUSPICIOUS

SUSPICION IS USUALLY based on one of three things. It can be an intuitive hunch, your own trust issues, or a past pattern of behavior when the person in question has a history of screwing up.

Take, for instance, Crystal and Jimmy. Crystal loved Jimmy. In fact, she was pregnant with their first child. Her relationship with men over the years had left her with many trust issues. Even though they had a great relationship, there was something about Jimmy that Crystal could feel in her heart wasn't being authentically expressed.

One afternoon, after a fiery argument, Jimmy stormed out of the house to get some space. Crystal then decided to go to Jimmy's laptop and search for confirming proof about her gut feelings. Sure enough, she found an email that he had sent to a mutual friend saying that he didn't know if he could trust himself to be faithful if he went away to a business conference. Crystal's heart felt broken. She was carrying their child! After just one tiny exploration into an email on a computer, she was guided to the truth.

Remember

MY ADVICE IS that you don't invade someone's privacy. My other piece of advice is that if you don't trust someone, and you are looking for ways to spy on them, then there is a massive need to open up the lines of love and communication. It's important to never do things deliberately that your partner would feel hurt by.

If you are a person who feels suspicious, allow this to be your meditation:

Dear Universe,

I release feelings of suspicion. I trust that all is well, and my intuition is always guiding me to see a higher perspective. May truth be my guiding light.
So be it, so it is.

16: Connected · 47: Honest · 90: Trusting

 **TENSE**

IN TODAY'S BUSY world, tension is commonly experienced by many people. It can manifest emotionally or physically, and it's usually caused by stress and anxiety. The good news is that there is so much you can do in order to move through this experience quickly.

Meditation is a great way to get out of your head and into your heart. It's been proven to relieve stress and tension, and it also helps to calm and soothe the sympathetic nervous system.

Remember

IF YOU FEEL tense, you must actively seek out ways to relax and connect to what's important. If it's family or relationship tension, then set some healthy boundaries.

Tension is something that needs to be defused in your life. Self-care rituals should be an extremely important element of your daily routine. Perhaps take a bath, get a massage, cook a healthy meal, or listen to relaxing music — seek joy wherever you can in order to alleviate the energy of tension.

As a place to begin, try this as your meditation:

Remove this tension from my body and my mind. May I now release this energy from my cells so that I feel vibrant, energized, and whole.
So be it, so it is.

10: Calm · 45: Healed · 99: Whole

(78) TERRIFIED

IN MELBOURNE, AUSTRALIA, trams are the main public transport system for moving people around the city. When I was about 19, I was on my way home from shopping. I got on the tram. The seats are in groups of four, so people are facing one another. The tram was crowded, and when I was finding a seat I heard this guy yelling:

"Tell your bitch to sit down or I'll shoot her."

The guy had a gun in his jacket pocket and he was pointing it directly at me. He was clearly under the influence of drugs. I kept my head down and did as he said. I sat next to the guy who the gunman was addressing. We sat in silence, crammed in with a whole bunch of other people, not knowing how the situation was going to play out. I felt terrified. Was this going to be a hostage situation? Was I going to get hurt? My heart was racing so fast. For eight stops I virtually held my breath. Then the guy sitting next to me grabbed my hand as if I was his girlfriend, and we fled as fast as we could out the doors of the tram.

Remember

WHEN YOU FEEL terrified, focus on your breathing to try and calm yourself down. Keep your awareness focused on your surroundings to stay safe at all times.

Dear Universe,

May my awareness be anchored into the present moment.
I ask that this feeling of being terrified be replaced with feeling cool, calm, and collected. I trust that everything will unfold as it should.
So be it, so it is.

4: Aware · 8: Brave · 10: Calm

 # TIRED

I DIDN'T SLEEP for the first five years of my son's life. Thomas would wake up every two hours. When he finally did start sleeping through the night, I gave birth to my daughter and the cycle began again. I was so tired, so very, very tired.

We go through many different phases in our lives. In one phase we might feel very vibrant and energetic. In another, you could feel as exuberant as a flat tire. The awareness of being tired is your soul calling you to get some rest.

There is a condition known as "adrenal fatigue," meaning that your body has been in "fight or flight" mode for a long period of time and your energy stores are all exhausted and burned-out.

Remember

A POWER NAP for ten minutes can become your best friend. Self-care is extremely important when you feel burned-out and tired.

Don't try to mask the problem with coffee or other caffeinated drinks; allow yourself to get some rest. Ask The Universe to recharge you with a sleeping meditation . . .

Dear Universe,

I ask that I now be placed into a deep and restorative sleep. During that time I trust that my cells, my organs, my mind, and my spirit are being energized and healed. May I wake up feeling fresh, revived, and ready for the beauty of life. **So be it, so it is.**

3: Aligned · 5: Balanced · 26: Energized

80 TRAPPED

MANY PEOPLE ARE unhappy or dissatisfied with their lives, and a lot of these people think that they have no control over their lives or what happens to them. However, you have the power to change your own life when you feel trapped.

You might feel trapped by circumstances that feel oppressive and unfair. It's a sad reality that not everyone has been dealt the same hand of cards in life. However, it's how we celebrate the differences that creates freedom.

There are people from all walks of life who have risen above feeling trapped by society, history, persecution, circumstance, and injustice. I deeply honor the souls who have traveled or are still traveling this path.

Remember

FEELING TRAPPED IS the natural desire for freedom rising within you. It's time to use your voice, lead with love, educate with compassion, and create an exit strategy for yourself.

Sometimes being restricted in different areas of our lives can help us to seek freedom faster, once we give ourselves permission to do so. Sometimes all you need to do is gain the different perspective that you have more freedom than you thought, because there are millions of people out there in the world who fight for the most basic of human rights on a daily basis.

The Universe wants you feel expansive, free, and released from the constructs of imprisonment you have created in your mind . . .

Dear Universe,

I am free. Through my empowered choices on a moment-by-moment basis,
I remember the expansive and all-pervading essence of my soul.
Feeling trapped is my call to spread my wings and fly.
So be it, so it is.

25: Empowered · 29: Expansive · 36: Free

81 TRAUMATIZED

TRAUMA IS NOT something to take lightly. Experiencing or witnessing something that changes the emotional landscape of who you are is a very profound invitation from The Universe to seek a path to healing. There are some things that you just can't undo or unsee. You might be haunted by these events in your mind and in your heart. The good news is that you can rewire your associations to the pain and live a life of emotional freedom.

Remember

LETTING GO OF pain does not mean that you forgive and forget. You must honor your role in the experience as part of your soul's journey.

The Universe will never give you more than you can handle. One powerful key is to remove anything that upsets you. Whether you need to physically remove something from your environment or cut ties to a person who reminds you of your past — it's okay.

PTSD (post-traumatic stress disorder) is real. The hormones, cells, and chemicals in your body need gentle recovery. Thankfully, The Universe is always present to hold your hand and heal your heart.

Dear Universe,

I am grateful for today. All that exists is now.
May I find joy in my day-to-day life and appreciate all the support and guidance
that I am offered. A problem shared is a problem spared.
So be it, so it is.

30: Expressive · 60: Nourished · 97: Vulnerable

82 TRIGGERED

FEELING TRIGGERED? IT might have been something you saw on social media or TV that you labeled as "wrong." It could be a video that reminded you of a traumatic experience. It could be a person who has a voice that sounds like fingernails on a chalkboard — the tone and timbre irritate you relentlessly. It could be a song on the radio that ignites bad memories. All of the senses can be emotionally triggered at various points in your life, activating memories and negative responses. More than likely it's because someone has said or done something that disrupts your own set of internal rules.

Remember

YOUR JOURNEY THROUGH life will always present you with triggers to rise above.

You are on a sacred mission from The Universe to grow and expand your soul.

Arguments and disagreements within relationships are usually where the triggers like to make an appearance. Your spouse might know how and where to drop the emotional bombs that will set you off. It's so easy to forget that your role is to rise above it and own your energy. Once you learn how to meet the triggers with compassion and no reaction, then the quality of your life will improve significantly.

When you feel triggered, please pause and ask The Universe for guidance:

Dear Universe,

Remind me to hold compassion in this situation.
I have the power to guide my energy and to choose the way to respond. May my words wield kindness as I move forward into a space of love.
So be it, so it is.

8: Brave · 14: Compassionate · 97: Vulnerable

 # UGLY

FEELING UGLY IS unnecessary. There is no such thing as being ugly! As human beings, we are all unique, and not a single one of us can be unequivocally deemed "unsightly." If you feel unattractive, consider tapping into the power of affirmations and remembering your true beauty. I've been teaching my daughter Lulu about multidimensional beauty. She is beautiful in her actions and her intentions, and that manifests outwardly no matter what she looks like. I get her to affirm her beauty every single day. In fact, I do this with all three of my daughters.

However, behavior can be ugly, so let's talk about that for a moment.

Situations, actions, reactions, etc. can fall into the realm of ugliness. I know that when I fight with my mother that things can get ugly really quickly! In the past we have both resorted to taking the low road, instead of the high road. Insults get thrown — labels, blame, accusations — and it's all less than desirable! Ugly behavior is underhanded and needs to be identified and managed as soon as it is spotted.

Remember

YOU ARE RESPONSIBLE for how you behave and respond to people and experiences. Always remember to be kind, no matter what. Kind words are never wasted.

Dear Universe,

I ask that feelings of ugliness now be released. May I remember to shine my inner beauty from within. I am a radiant soul, radiating a vibrant form. I am kind, compassionate, and caring.
So be it, so it is.

6: Beautiful · 15: Confident · 95: Vibrant

(84) UNCERTAIN

IF YOU'RE FEELING the sting of uncertainty in your life, then you are fully engaged in one of the most powerful lessons that life has to offer. We've all heard the saying that there are only two things that are certain in life: death and taxes. Everything else is a movable feast that can be exhilarating and terrifying at the same time. The difference is how you view your situation as it unfolds.

In 2014, I was pregnant for the third time in six months. I'd previously lost a couple of tiny heartbeats and felt so afraid. I was about eight weeks pregnant when Sean and I went to have an ultrasound to see how the baby was growing because I was bleeding.

"It doesn't look good, but there's a heartbeat. Come back in two weeks," the doctor said.

During that time Sean printed out hundreds of different posts on pregnancy forums that had stories from women who had experienced slow-growth babies, and everything turned out fine.

My dear friend Dallyce reminded me that as long as there is life, there's hope.

I used these pieces of inspiration to anchor into my awareness that everything would be okay. I was riding a massive wave of uncertainty. It was a powerful spiritual lesson.

Remember

IF YOU CAN get comfortable with uncertainty and view it as part of a divine plan, then you will gracefully navigate your way through life and any situation you are presented with.

At around 11 weeks, I lost that baby. The lab tests revealed that it was a girl with a rare genetic disorder called trisomy 18. Had she survived, she would have died within weeks. The experience and the honor of carrying her tiny life was worth every microsecond of uncertainty.

When (not if) you are faced with uncertainty, allow The Universe to hold your hand and guide you to remember the following:

Dear Universe,

I am fully present in this moment. My soul remembers that getting comfortable with uncertainty is my sacred contract and I embrace the opportunity to experience the beautiful fullness of life.
So be it, so it is.

8: Brave · 86: Surrendered · 90: Trusting

85 UNGRATEFUL

IT WAS CHRISTMAS morning 1986, and my little sister and I were opening presents from our parents. My sister got something called "My Child," which is the doll that everyone at school wanted at the time — myself included. You'd press a button on its neck and it would hug you. I opened up my gift and it was an "Alf" doll (you know, the weird TV sitcom alien from the planet Melmac), and I instantly complained instead of being grateful.

"It's not even a talking Alf doll! I wanted a My Child!"

I'm sure I sounded like Veruca Salt from Charlie and Chocolate Factory, only more entitled and brattish.

You see, when you are in a space of not taking time to be grateful, then you are telling The Universe not to send anything else in your direction. Being ungrateful is the fastest way not to manifest transformation into your reality.

Remember

TO COUNTERACT THE effects of being ungrateful, look for things to appreciate.

The next time you catch yourself in the space of being ungrateful, remember that everything that shows up in your life is a gift, even if it's an Alf doll . . .

Dear Universe,

Remind me of all the things in my life that I can be grateful for.
May I create a daily practice of appreciation so that I can fully embrace everything and anything that I manifest.
So be it, so it is.

41: Grateful · 76: Satisfied · 87: Thoughtful

 UNHAPPY

> "All human unhappiness comes from not facing
> reality squarely, exactly as it is."
> — BUDDHA

IF YOU'RE FEELING unhappy you must ask yourself the following powerful question:

What does my soul need right now?

There are millions upon millions of people in the world who need to experience more happiness in their daily lives. The fabulous news is that if you break it down into moments of allowing yourself to experience happiness, then all of those moments will string together to create a beautiful life of contentment.

Remember

YOUR LIFE WILL thrive when you take responsibility and ownership of your happiness. It's not up to others to make you happy.

If you're unhappy, make it your sole mission to seek more joy in your life. A daily practice of gratitude will also radically transform your reality. Write in your journal three things you're grateful for each day and watch the magic manifest into your life.

For a decent chunk of my 20s I was pretty miserable. But then I literally trained myself to find even the smallest things to appreciate. I would then start to catch myself in moments where I thought, "I'm so happy right now." This practice, as simplistic as it is, creates a massive amount of emotional freedom.

For example, if you're unhappy with the service at a restaurant, unhappy that your partner didn't get you a gift for your anniversary, or unhappy that someone ate the last doughnut in the box, stop yourself in those moments where you feel disgruntled and reshape your reality with your feelings. Choose your battles wisely. The feeling of unhappiness is a major signal to The Universe to deliver more things to feel unhappy about. If you can stop the feeling from escalating, then you win at the game of seeking happiness.

Dear Universe,

Reveal to me the exquisite continuum of happiness that I always have access to anytime I remember. May I create a slideshow in my mind of the happiest times in my life, and may they act as a reminder that I get to choose how I guide my feelings in each and every beautiful moment of my life.
So be it, so it is.

17: Content · 44: Happy · 80: Serene

87 UNHEARD

"YOU'RE NOT LISTENING to me! You're not hearing what I'm saying."

Sound familiar?

When you feel like someone is not hearing you, it can be upsetting. The first couple of ways to make sure that you are heard is to ask yourself if you are indeed being a good listener. Sometimes we unknowingly project the way we are behaving onto others. If you know it to be true that someone really isn't hearing what you are saying, then you might need to switch up your tactics to meet the person where they are. People have many different modes of receiving information. Some of us hear. Some of us see. Some of us feel the information we are being presented with.

If you are communicating with a visual-style learner you must try to "show" your key points. A kinesthetic person (a feelings-based learner) needs to hear words that include a more tactile approach; they use statements such as: "I feel," etc. For the audio-based learner, your tone is imperative; if you are too loud or aggressive, you will not be creating the optimal space to be heard.

Remember

A MESSAGE DELIVERED doesn't always mean that the message has been received.

When I was married to Max, I knew that the only time I could really talk to him was when he was driving the car. We rarely exchanged eye contact, and no matter what I presented visually, tonally, or by expressing my feelings, I was usually left feeling unheard. The key point to remember is that if your message isn't being received, then maybe it's not meant to at that point in time. Also, remember not to take it personally, or it will drive you a little nutty.

Turn to The Universe to remind you of your strength to communicate:

Dear Universe,

May I remember that I have the power to bridge communication.
May I be guided to deliver my message or information where it will be received
with an open heart and an open mind.
So be it, so it is.

4: Aware · 43: Guided · 46: Helpful

UNLOVED

FEELING UNLOVED IS sad, but it's an illusion. You are so loved, valued, worthy, and cherished.

Remember

IF YOU FEEL unloved, please know that The Universe loves and adores you unconditionally.

Something that most people don't know about me is that my first husband and I had two wedding ceremonies. The second one was when I was bruised from abuse and pregnant, and we did it so I could take on his surname.

However, the first one was at a spiritual meditation retreat in New Zealand. We were surrounded by friends. Our wedding was officiated by my meditation teacher, Bhai Sahib Ji. I was just 20 years old and so excited to be finally connecting with Max on a deeper level. It was a spontaneous idea that the group came up with in order to make our union official.

We drove into the local town to buy matching gold rings. We got dressed up. We had an "ultra-spiritual" wedding ceremony with the beautiful sound of the ocean behind us. All of our friends pitched in to buy us the honeymoon suite at a local hotel to celebrate our new marriage. They decorated the bed in rose petals, and there was champagne. All we had to do was celebrate our soul union. And yet, I waited in bed for hours until I finally fell asleep. Max just wanted to watch television. There was no romance or fireworks. Just TV. I felt so unloved, unseen, and unworthy. It should have been a red flag that something was not right.

Sometimes in my mind's eye, I travel back in time to send love to that 20-year-old girl who craved to be loved. I want to remind her that The Universe had a plan and that that space of feeling unloved manifested true love, eventually.

Dear Universe,

I am loved. I am cherished. Remind me that my spirit is in alignment with the essence of all that I desire. May I treat myself in the way that I wish to be treated by my loved ones.
So be it, so it is.

12: Cherished · 54: Loved · 100: Worthy

 # 89 UNSAFE

IF YOU FEEL unsafe right now, please reach out to someone for support or assistance. Feeling unsafe is scary, so you need to calm yourself as much as possible and do your best to feel okay right now. Sometimes we feel unsafe on an ongoing basis. Make sure that your safety becomes a priority and that you're not placing yourself in harm's way.

If you are feeling safe right now, please commit this advice to your memory because it could become helpful when you need it.

One evening, Sean and I were in Melbourne, Australia. It was after 1 a.m. and we were walking back to our hotel past the Flinders Street train station. There were not many people around. Two big guys were walking toward us aggressively, like they had the intention to mug us. Sean and I both felt unsafe. At the same time Sean and I kept our energy calm, we stood a little taller, and walked a little more briskly. Because we showed that we weren't intimidated by the thugs, they walked straight by us. Two days later there were reports of a couple being stabbed in that same area of the train station.

Remember

IF YOU FEEL unsafe, think on your feet. Be aware of your surroundings, your energy, and your escape path. Be prepared.

Dear Universe,

Allow me to feel safe where I'm at right now. May I trust that my intuition and gut feelings will guide me to safety in all situations I am faced with.
So be it, so it is.

8: Brave · 10: Calm · 75: Safe

MARGOT, A WOMAN in her mid-40s, could eat seven plates of food at a buffet and never feel full. One of her hobbies was to leave critical reviews on Yelp of the restaurants she visited. In fact, she frequently left one-star reviews on Amazon, iTunes, and anywhere else that offered the space to express dissatisfaction. On Facebook, her favorite button was the angry face.

Remember

IF YOU ARE constantly complaining about what shows up in your reality, The Universe will send you more to complain about.

The truth about Margo is a very sad story. It's a story I've heard thousands of times from my manifesting students around the world. As a young child, Margot had a very abusive mother who told her that nothing was ever good enough. As a result, Margot felt unworthy of experiencing joy and contentment. It was a pattern that had been established since early childhood. Nothing would ever be good enough.

One day Margot decided to rise above the pain she was experiencing. The weight of releasing her beliefs around perfectionism led to her losing over 40 pounds! She manifested her soulmate. She stopped leaving bad reviews and switched her focus to things to be grateful for.

The truth is that feeling unsatisfied is a call from your higher self to feel worthy and to accept your reality as it is. This is where you meet the magic and begin to play with it . . .

Dear Universe,

I ask that I may be grateful for whatever shows up in my reality. May I now fill up my heart with the energy of joy, love, laughter, and light so that I can feel content and peaceful in this moment.
So be it, so it is.

20: Delighted · 76: Satisfied · 100: Worthy

91 UNSEEN

MAX WAS THE caretaker of a meditation center. I was 20 and he was 32. After the group sessions ended in the evenings, I would stick around to see if Max wanted me to spend the night. We'd been dating for about seven months, and I was still naively and patiently waiting for our romance to get interesting. It was kind of like watching a movie that you're aware takes a while to get into, and yet you know the end of the movie is close, and you've wasted your time.

One evening, Max was washing spinach in the kitchen sink with his back turned to me. As a man of few words, he said:

"Should we get married?"

This was not exactly the Disney Princess version of a proposal I had mapped out in my mind.

"Yes!" I beamed.

Even after seven months, my self-worth was pretty low. I made the foolish assumption this proposal was a sign that Max was ready to come out of his shell once and for all.

The weird thing was that he didn't look at me when he proposed. He didn't stare into my eyes and see my soul. He was washing spinach in the kitchen sink! Then, after dinner was made, he decided that he would build a model plane out of balsa wood. I sat and watched. You can't make this stuff up! I felt so unseen. Can you imagine what not being seen does to your psyche? How it impacts your confidence over time?

Remember

IF YOU FEEL unseen in any area of your life and you allow that to happen, please find a mirror, stare into your own beautiful eyes, and say: "I SEE YOU."

Work with The Universe to truly call in people who see the magnificent soul that you are. Meditate on this:

Dear Universe,

I am worthy of being seen. Empower my spirit with
the intention of visibility so that I can shine my light and connect
with others on an authentic level that nourishes my soul.
So be it, so it is.

77: Seen · 96: Visible · 100: Worthy

 # UNSETTLED

FEELING UNSETTLED IS the exact opposite of feeling that you're secured in your current reality. You could be living out of a suitcase, couch surfing, living with your parents, dealing with a partner who travels a lot, or you might be traveling.

There's an energy of instability. There's the persistent knowing the foundation beneath your reality at the moment is fluid and somewhat transient. It's movable, changeable, and the wind could shift direction at any moment.

Remember

THE UNIVERSE IS training you to become comfortable with uncertainty. Feeling unsettled is indicative of the energy of change sweeping through your reality.

There will come a time when you feel grounded, peaceful, and stable in your situation no matter what you are experiencing. However, you must always hold the awareness in your heart that nothing (meaning "no thing") is permanent. You are always safe and settled in the present moment and in this understanding you can ask The Universe to remind you . . .

Dear Universe,

Reveal to me a sense of stability within the uncertainty.
Remind me that the nature of life is transient and that feeling
settled is a state of awareness within my soul.
So be it, so it is.

33: Flowing · 61: Open · 75: Safe

 **USED**

"HE SAID HE'S going to leave his wife once and for all! I just want to be able to believe him this time. He says he loves me."

This was the exact statement that had been expressed dozens of times by Joanne. It almost seemed to be as cyclic as the phases of the moon. She'd doubt the validity and viability of her relationship with James — a financial adviser — and then feel like her entire soul was set on fire with passion when he requested a secret weekend away with her.

For five years, Joanne's closest friends told her she was being used. In no way was she open to seeing the situation for what it was. Then she found out she was pregnant, and James told her to "get rid of it" because his wife was pregnant as well.

It's important to remember that relationships are mutual support systems.

Remember

WHEN YOUR NEEDS are not being met, and your values are compromised, it's time to move on from allowing yourself to be used.

Take your power back and nurture your awareness of necessary boundaries with this meditation:

I stand strong in my understanding that I will no longer allow myself to be taken advantage of. I draw a very deep line in the cosmic sands of intention. May it not be crossed and may it be lovingly protected.
So be it, so it is.

32: Fierce · 84: Strong · 94: Valued

 # USELESS

IF YOU ARE feeling useless, please know that The Universe is calling you to rise up and be of service to others. This is the fastest way to improve your self-esteem and spark the magic of contribution. The lifeblood of humanity is built upon being of service to others.

Remember

FEELING USELESS IS a sacred reminder that you are worthy of anything that your heart desires because you are an incredible and unique human being.

You might have moments when you believe the illusion that you have nothing to give, no purpose, and no role to play on the beautiful stage of life. It's not true! Every single person who occupies this planet has been assigned a sacred mission. Your role is to follow your joy and unravel the path to freedom that is uniquely yours and yours alone to decide.

Dear Universe,

Guide me on how I may be of service to others in this world.
May it be a reminder that I am a valuable and cherished member of my community and my circle of loved ones, and may it honor the core essence of my sacred assignment here on Earth.
So be it, so it is.

3: Aligned · 37: Generous · 92: Unique

 **VULNERABLE**

BEING VULNERABLE ACTIVATES magic within relationships—both personal and professional. The willingness to be truly open and honest about how you're feeling and what you've experienced is a gift. It took me many years to feel brave enough to share from a space of vulnerability. In fact, there have been several moments throughout this book where I have questioned if I'm being too vulnerable.

It can be scary, but when you open up to people and share from an authentic space of experience, it empowers others who resonate with your story.

Remember

WHEN YOU CAN be unguarded with your heart, mind, and soul, this builds trust and reminds people that we're all in this together.

Vulnerability is the surrender of control and personal power in regard to letting someone get close to you and form a connection.

For ten years I only told a handful of people about the abuse in my first marriage. I kept it from my family and I hid the shame inside. My freedom was found when I discovered that sharing my story from a space of vulnerability actually helped other people in similar situations. I became the person that I needed in my darkest hour—this is how the essence of true leadership is sparked.

If you are debating whether or not being vulnerable will help you or hinder you, turn to The Universe for this guidance:

Dear Universe,

I ask that my feelings of vulnerability are strengthened so
I can share my perspective and experience to inspire others. Show me how
I may be of service and how my past had a purpose.
So be it, so it is.

15: Confident · 42: Grounded · 75: Safe

 **WIRED**

CAN'T SLEEP? FEELING restless? Too much coffee? Too much screen time before bed?

When you are struggling to relax, unwind, and unplug, then it's time to slow down and focus on getting out of your head and into feeling grounded in your body.

It's super important to focus on your breath.

Remember

OUR BREATH IS always a very helpful resource to check to see if we're incredibly wired and hyper, or relaxing into the steady pace of each moment.

If all else fails, try taking a hot bath or pouring yourself a nice glass of red wine.

Try this meditation when you are eager to defuse your haywire energy:

Dear Universe,

May I now take a deep breath in and hold it. Upon exhaling,
I release any frantic energy I am storing in my body. I inhale the energy of relaxation. I exhale wired energy and release it with love. Breathe in the full energy of awareness within the present moment.
So be it, so it is.

42: Grounded · 71: Relaxed · 73: Rested

⟨97⟩ WITHDRAWN

WHEN YOU'RE DEPRESSED, or not feeling like your usual best, you slowly withdraw into yourself. You don't go out and do the things that you loved to do before, you stop reaching out to friends, you lose your confidence, and you feel like hiding.

More than likely you're slowing down because you can't find the energy to do anything. The good news is that it's perfectly okay to withdraw from aspects of your life at various times. It becomes a little concerning when you can't function.

Remember

LIFE IS NOT a dress rehearsal. You don't get another chance to live a life of happiness and joy. The time is NOW!

In order to rise above feeling withdrawn you need to be very gentle with yourself. Take one step at a time, and each of those steps needs to be in the direction of doing something that you love. There's a reason that solitary confinement is the worst form of punishment in the prison systems. It's because the body, mind, and spirit complex requires human contact, support, and connection in order to thrive.

When you can identify that you feel withdrawn, turn to The Universe to coax you out of your cave . . .

Dear Universe,

I give myself full permission to be gentle and kind in order to nurture a space for healing in every area of my life. I am open to attracting the right people who will support me unconditionally — in times when I need a hug or in times when I require some space.

So be it, so it is.

16: Connected · 67: Present · 75: Safe

 # WORRIED

> "Worry often gives a small thing a big shadow."
> — SWEDISH PROVERB

THE FEELING OF worry calls to be dealt with on a moment-by-moment basis. The weird pangs of anxiety in the pit of your stomach are The Universe's way of asking you to have faith that everything is unfolding as it should. Most worry and concern usually doesn't amount to anything. However, sometimes it does, and this is the movable and transformative nature of life. What will move you through this experience is the courage you hold in your heart.

Remember

IF YOU ARE worried, you are activating the energy of fear. This feeling needs to be replaced with trust in The Universe, even in the face of extreme uncertainty.

It was 1 a.m. on October 1, 2017 and my baby daughter Ava woke me up. I opened my eyes and grabbed my phone to see what time it was. I had over a hundred messages from people saying they were "worried" about me. The day before, I had posted photos on Instagram from the Mandalay Bay resort in Las Vegas. News reports were surfacing that a massacre had taken place from the same hotel.

Twitter was giving mixed reports of multiple casinos with multiple shooters.

I woke up Sean to let him know. We sat outside on our balcony, which overlooks the iconic Las Vegas skyline. There was not a single plane or helicopter in the sky. It was so silent, you could have heard a pin drop. Many of the lights of the city had been turned off or dimmed. The eerie mix of concern and silence was palpable. We didn't feel safe, and we were so worried for the safety of the people in the buildings we could see from a distance.

If you are worried about someone or something, then meditate with The Universe to guide your energy and send the essence of support in their direction . . .

Dear Universe,

I release feelings of worry and concern and trust in the process
of transformation. May I now dedicate and direct the energy of love, light,
wellness, and wholeness to the people who need it right now. The essence of
support and well-being surrounds me and my loved ones.
So be it, so it is.

29: Expansive · 33: Flowing · 84: Strong

99 WORTHLESS

THERE IS A strong connection between the relationship we have with food and the relationship we have with our sense of self. There are even some schools of thought that believe that your connection to food is your connection to The Universe. How you nourish yourself has everything to do with feeling worthy. When you feel worthless, you tend to sabotage your efforts to heal from within. This is where addiction is birthed and tremendous emotional upheaval is unleashed.

"Who would love you with that ugly spare tire around your middle? You're fat. You're ugly. You're old."

Max would say this to me during our fights. I was 116 pounds and 23 years old. I felt so worthless. I would cook, clean, and take care of the children, and my role in the household was still deemed meaningless. I would often joke that I could set myself on fire and Max wouldn't notice.

My feelings of worthlessness manifested as an eating disorder. I would eat, make myself throw up, and lie to my husband about having already eaten. Bingeing and purging was the only activity that made me feel as if I were in control of my life. Feeling worthless triggered ways to harm myself behind closed doors. After all, there was no space for me to ask for my needs to be met. This compounded the shame of the abuse cycle.

This destructive internal energy still rises up from time to time. Experiences can unfold that create the perfect storm for old patterns of feeling worthless to arise. The key is to be mindful and to steer away from the illusion that you are not enough.

Remember

YOU ARE WORTHY. **The Universe chose you to be here.**
Meditate on the following:

Dear Universe,

Give me the clarity to rise above the illusion that I am not enough.
Empower me to remember I am worthy. I am worthy of anything my heart desires.
So be it, so it is.

25: Empowered · 43: Guided · 100: Worthy

 **WOUNDED**

ONE OF MY all-time favorite quotes is by the Sufi poet Rumi:

"The wound is the place where the light enters you."

When you feel wounded — whether it's emotionally, physically, or spiritually — Universal energy is called forth to heal you if you allow it. Your role is to facilitate the healing or let the wound define who you are. Moving through this time might leave you feeling a little stuck and sometimes a little raw.

I find myself so fascinated by a few people I see at the gym who have prosthetic limbs. There's this one guy with a mechanical leg from the knee down. There's a strong and powerful energy about him — how he moves, how he lifts weights, and how he is committed to showing up to the gym each day. Keep in mind I have never met this guy, but I can intuitively feel that he has healed some intense mental barriers to show up in the way that he does. Quite often there are many extraordinary and inspiring people who have been through horrendous experiences to get to where they are today. I like to watch TEDx talks to remind me of the potential to transform pain into power.

So whatever your pain is right now, or your "wound," just know that it is a portal to possibility.

 *Remember*

EVERYTHING YOU ARE going through right now is preparing you for what you asked for. Your reality today is the crystallized emotions of yesterday.

 *Dear Universe,*

May I welcome and accept the energy of healing to help guide me through this time. I trust in the infinite wisdom of my body, my mind, and my spirit to restore balance and harmony to my being.

So be it, so it is.

25: Empowered · 45: Healed · 89: Transformative

Part 3

100 MINI-MEDITATIONS TO EMBRACE LOVE

When you appreciate, give thanks, and celebrate how you feel in the present moment, you invite more magic to manifest into your life. Whether you want to feel the love or you are in the process of guiding your energy in a new direction, The Universe within you is always ready to support and guide you on your journey.

The love that you allow yourself to experience is based in direct proportion to the amount of appreciation you hold in your heart and the amount of love you are willing to give.

In this section, you will ask yourself again:

HOW DO I *feel* RIGHT NOW? HOW DO I *want* TO *feel* ?

EACH "LOVE-BASED" FEELING will have a story or a piece of inspiration or wisdom followed by a "Dear Universe" mini-meditation. Tune in to the energy of each love-based theme and call it into your life on a new and vibrant level.

1. Abundant	17. Content	33. Flowing
2. Adored	18. Creative	34. Focused
3. Aligned	19. Dedicated	35. Forgiving
4. Aware	20. Delighted	36. Free
5. Balanced	21. Devoted	37. Generous
6. Beautiful	22. Divine	38. Gentle
7. Blissful	23. Eager	39. Graceful
8. Brave	24. Elated	40. Gracious
9. Brilliant	25. Empowered	41. Grateful
10. Calm	26. Energized	42. Grounded
11. Cheerful	27. Enlightened	43. Guided
12. Cherished	28. Enthusiastic	44. Happy
13. Clear	29. Expansive	45. Healed
14. Compassionate	30. Expressive	46. Helpful
15. Confident	31. Festive	47. Honest
16. Connected	32. Fierce	48. Hopeful

49. Infinite

50. Inquisitive

51. Inspired

52. Intuitive

53. Joyful

54. Loved

55. Loving

56. Lucky

57. Magical

58. Motivated

59. Moved

60. Nourished

61. Open

62. Passionate

63. Peaceful

64. Playful

65. Positive

66. Powerful

67. Present

68. Prosperous

69. Protected

70. Proud

71. Relaxed

72. Relieved

73. Rested

74. Reverent

75. Safe

76. Satisfied

77. Seen

78. Selfless

79. Sensual

80. Serene

81. Sexy

82. Soothed

83. Still

84. Strong

85. Supported

86. Surrendered

87. Thoughtful

88. Tolerant

89. Transformative

90. Trusting

91. Unashamed

92. Unique

93. Uplifted

94. Valued

95. Vibrant

96. Visible

97. Vulnerable

98. Welcomed

99. Whole

100. Worthy

① ABUNDANT

WHEN YOU FEEL abundant, you are tuned in to the energy of freedom and limitless possibilities. It feels like a warm day in spring after a long and drawn-out winter. You might have a grounded and mindful sense of knowing that all is well in the present moment, and that it's just going to get better from this point onward.

Remember

ABUNDANCE CAN BE defined on your own terms.

It could be financial freedom, or the ease of trusting that The Universe will always deliver assistance in your time of need. It could also be symbolized by resources that are plentiful, such as growing your own vegetables, the gift of drinking clean water, a friend cooking you a meal, or manifesting a fresh bouquet of flowers.

Abundance is everywhere when you are dialed into seeking things to appreciate. As the New Thought teacher Florence Scovel Shinn once said, "There is supply for every demand."

This means that every desire you have is met with the energy of possibility. Once you remember this truth and anchor it into your memory you can begin to play with the opportunities The Universe sends your way.

Let this be your meditation to manifest the energy of abundance into your life:

Dear Universe,

Thank you for the abundance that is effortlessly flowing into my life in various different ways. Thank you for the opportunity to see money as energy. May I be guided to remember the power of gratitude. May I be inspired to give back to causes that contribute to the greater good. May I trust that there is a limitless source of prosperity, always. Thank you for the freedom that has manifested into my life.

So be it, so it is.

② ADORED

WHAT MAKES YOU feel adored? Whether it's a romantic gesture from your lover or when a dear friend remembers your birthday, how you receive that love affects whether or not you manifest more of it. If you can't accept gestures of affection, it can create tension in your relationship. However, if you embrace the energy of being adored then it opens the floodgates to a wondrous world of possibilities for you to feel loved and valued.

When I met and fell in love with my soulmate, Sean, it was terribly difficult for me to learn how to accept his adoration. I was so fiercely independent that I wasn't able to trust that the love he was showing me was real. Slowly but surely, I allowed myself to be adored, to be treated like the queen of the household. You see, when you're in a relationship — whether it's a marriage, a union, a friendship, partnership, or agreement — it's a mutual support system. You must be open to expressing appreciation. To do this, it's important that you allow yourself to receive the love in return. This helps the flow of energy keep moving and expanding the strength and viability of the relationship.

Remember

THE KEY PIECE of wisdom is that The Universe adores you unconditionally.

Everyone is adored! You are a magnificent human being, and you are uniquely you. Getting to a space where you can genuinely open your heart to be adored is something to celebrate. Most people push away love and kindness because they don't feel worthy. Celebrate that you are willing to receive.

Let this be your empowering reminder to welcome adoration:

> *Dear Universe,*
>
> I am open to receiving love and kindness. My heart is full of gratitude
> for the surprises, kind gestures, miracles, and expressions of affection that
> show up in my reality.
> **So be it, so it is.**

③ ALIGNED

WHEN YOU TUNE in to the goals, dreams, wishes, and desires that you intend to manifest into your reality, the key point is to align your energy and your vibration with what you want. This means that you place yourself in the energetic field of possibilities. For instance, in Florence Scovel Shinn's book *The Magic Path of Intuition*, she states that if you want to attract a million dollars, you need to get comfortable with a million dollars. You must get into the feeling space to experience alignment.

One afternoon, not too long after Sean and I moved to the US from Australia in 2015, we decided that it could be fun to go to an open house viewing of a 7 million dollar mansion for sale in our neighborhood. For impact, the realtor had a brand-new Lamborghini parked out front so that potential buyers could have a cheesy photo moment. I immediately felt my issues of worthiness rise to the surface. I could face the situation with confidence, or I could choose to avoid the invitation to sit in the Lamborghini.

You can't sit in that car, Sarah! You're not important enough!

I decided not to listen to the inner voice that keeps me small. Instead I said: "In the name of alignment, I will sit in this million-dollar custom car and feel worthy."

After I did, it really wasn't such a big deal. I was thankful my mind could see the benefits of pushing through the limiting beliefs.

Remember

WHATEVER YOUR INTENTION, whether it's to manifest a million dollars or a ridiculously expensive car, to attract your soulmate, or even to find the perfect rental home, make sure you take time to feel aligned.

Dear Universe,

Thank you for this beautiful feeling of alignment. I trust that everything is in the perfect place to begin manifesting my goals, dreams, wishes, and desires. May I seek joy in every experience along my journey.
So be it, so it is.

AWARE

ONE OF MY dearest friends and mentors, Scott deMoulin, teaches the following piece of wisdom to his clients and students around the world:

"Awareness Precedes Understanding. Understanding Precedes Change."

This means that nothing will ever change in your life unless you become aware of the reasons something has to change. For example, our "Dear Universe" moments when we cry out for help are instances where awareness is at the forefront of our experience.

Throughout life, we peel back the different layers of awareness, almost as if we are peeling an onion. Each layer represents a different depth of understanding, at different times our lives. This is often accompanied by getting older and accumulating wisdom from our body of life experience.

Remember

WHEN YOU TRULY feel aware, you can catch yourself in a present moment of self-realization.

You remember the truth that spirituality and awareness is not a "one size fits all" solution. Our awareness arises from our understanding that as humans we never have it all figured out, and we're all on a journey to learn, grow, and pay attention to the reality that is being presented to us.

Take a few minutes to try this awareness meditation:

Dear Universe,

May I focus on my breath. May I become aware of the animated force within my body. May I become aware of the ways in which I can improve my life. May I hold awareness of the present moment.
So be it, so it is.

⑤ BALANCED

THE SIX ASPECTS to balance within your life are physical, mental, emotional, social, financial, and spiritual. If any one of these elements doesn't get tended to, it can create chaos in various areas of your experience. It can also create unnecessary pressure.

But here's what I believe: Balance is a myth — or perhaps even an illusion. The circus performer balancing on a tightrope takes very careful steps on that high wire because they could fall on either side at any given moment. Even nutritionists would say that eating a "varied" diet is better than eating a boring old "balanced" diet. When all areas of your life are perceived to be balanced, it can take the sparkle out of your daily experience. I can tell you with 100 percent confidence that with four children and three dogs and running a business, seeking balance flew out the window years ago and set me free. This doesn't mean that I don't strive for harmony, but if I had to measure the efficacy of balance in my life, I would probably need an intervention! Striking a work/life balance is sometimes tricky too. I'll be brushing my teeth at 10 p.m., and my husband and I will have an impromptu business meeting in our bathroom.

Remember
ENERGY GOES WHERE attention flows!

If seeking balance is important to you, that's totally fine — especially if you are just setting out on your spiritual journey. Just remember to go with the flow and to release rigidity and rules around ticking the balance boxes.

Dear Universe,

May I be guided to serve the different areas of my life
that need care and attention when I feel called to do so. May I trust and
surrender that balance is optional, and it's not 100 percent required all the time.
This awareness brings me a sense of peace and of freedom.
So be it, so it is.

6 BEAUTIFUL

YOU ARE SO beautiful! You are uniquely you inside and out. Feeling beautiful from within is so incredibly important. Inner beauty is where it's at, because there is a lot of cold, empty, vacuous, fake business going on in the world. You don't need to buy into the illusion of airbrushed, Photoshopped, carefully curated beauty. If you're reading these words, I know you can see through this. We are beautiful souls, radiating a beautiful form. The fabulous news is that you can define what is beautiful on your own terms. Flaws, scars, wrinkles, moles, dimples, and all . . . if you doubt your own beauty, just imagine for a moment how you would see yourself through the eyes of The Universe. What do you see? You are perfect. Look in the mirror and tell yourself how beautiful you are because your spirit chose to be here with us, playing in this super-fun playground called "life" at this point in time. You have so much to be grateful for.

If you have trouble with this process, try to avoid wishing that aspects of yourself would be different. When you do this, you create energetic resistance in your life. It literally creates a block in your flow of energy and prevents you from manifesting.

ACCEPTANCE AND CONFIDENCE are the keys to beauty.

May this be your meditation to celebrate your beauty:

Dear Universe,

Thank you for the gift of me. Just as no two snowflakes are the same, I celebrate my own uniqueness. May I inspire others to express their own essence of beauty.
So be it, so it is.

7 BLISSFUL

OH SWEET BLISS! It has miraculous superpowers to create a radical transformation that you never knew was possible.

Bliss can be experienced in your life in so many beautiful ways. From the pure energy of happiness when you hold a newborn baby in your arms to walking barefoot on the exquisite white sands of a tropical beach, bliss can be found in any place you choose to seek joy. The great Joseph Campbell once said:

"If you do follow your bliss, you put yourself on a kind of track that has been there all the while, waiting for you, and the life that you ought to be living is the one you are living. Follow your bliss and don't be afraid, and doors will open where you didn't know they were going to be."

Remember

WHEN YOU TUNE in to the energy of bliss, you raise your vibration and flow with the alignment of your desires.

Create your own "Dear Universe" #BlissList as your meditation. What are the things, people, places, or experiences that bring you the most joy in your life?

Dear Universe,

I openly welcome more bliss into my life on a daily basis. Thank you for the awareness to seek joy in anything I desire and everything I do.
So be it, so it is.

---

8 BRAVE

ACCORDING TO THE *Oxford English Dictionary* the word "brave" is defined as: "Ready to face and endure danger or pain; showing courage."

I'm not sure if this definition is accurate. I don't know of anyone who, when faced with a situation that requires bravery and strength, has felt "ready." I know from personal experience that true courage is summoned in those moments of unknown outcomes, when you must manage your energy without having solid proof that you'll be okay. When you are required to be brave, it feels like you are walking a fine line between "let's just get it over with" and "I'm not sure what's about to happen here."

Such experiences can be both terrifying and exhilarating at the same time, depending on your perspective.

Moments in my life that have required bravery, or my definition of it (standing strong, even when you don't feel ready), have been some of the most magical and transformative events in my life. Were they easy? No. But was it worth it? Yes.

From leaving a 10-year toxic marriage to fighting depression and battling poverty, I overcame each obstacle because I kept on pushing through despite the uncertainty. Giving up was not an option because I was motivated by love and, ultimately, survival.

The courage that you require to overcome any situation is always within you.

Remember
YOU ARE SO much stronger than you think you are.

Dear Universe,

May I be brave in the moments that require strength. Allow my heart to remember that I am never given more than I can handle.
So be it, so it is.

9 BRILLIANT

TUNE IN TO the energy of your own brilliance — we all have it within us. There is so much infinite wisdom and guidance that you have access to. You just need to believe and remember that you are capable of anything you set your mind and heart to. Think about this for a moment. How did Beethoven compose such famous pieces of music when he was deaf? How did Frida Kahlo recover from a near-fatal bus accident and continue to create such iconic works of art? How is it that J.K. Rowling received so many rejection letters for her book idea before Harry Potter became a household name? The reason is because people who achieve great success in life believe in their own brilliance. It doesn't need to be a pompous act of self-puffery, it just needs to be a tiny spark of inspiration that you carry inside your heart to remind you that you are worthy.

Remember

LIFE-CHANGING IDEAS THAT transform the landscape of humanity are often ideas that are "received" or "downloaded" from The Universe.

Be open to manifesting your brilliance by paying close attention to your dreams, cultivating your intuition, and trusting that the right circumstances will appear to support your intentions.

May this be your meditation to draw forth the essence of your brilliance:

Dear Universe,

Open my heart and my mind to receive the core essence
of my unique brilliance. May it manifest with clarity, specificity, and
steps to take inspired action when called to do so.
So be it, so it is.

10 CALM

WHEN YOU MANIFEST a state of feeling calm, no matter what your reality is presenting, you win. Your mission (should you choose to accept it) is to learn how to remain calm in the eye of the storm. Life can throw anything in your direction, and you will know that you can instantly go to your happy place and enjoy a sense of inner peace and tranquility. The fastest and easiest access point to this place is via meditation.

You can train yourself to feel calm when confronted with difficult situations.

Remember

THE MORE YOU integrate meditation into your daily spiritual practice, the more you strengthen your ability to keep calm and carry on.

If you desire to create the energy of tranquility and calmness, take a moment to visualize the following:

Dear Universe,

In my mind's eye I am now sitting in the meditation gardens
that overlook the ocean. The sunshine feels warm on my skin.
The air is fresh, and the sweet scent of jasmine flowers is being carried on the ocean breeze. All is well, and happiness and contentment fills my heart. I commit this feeling of stillness and calm to my subconscious mind. At any point I can bring myself back here to sit and reflect from a space of compassion and not from reaction. Thank you for this peace in my life.
So be it, so it is.

11 CHEERFUL

NORMA CLEANED THE bathrooms at the Red Rock Casino in Las Vegas. As you could imagine, Friday and Saturday nights saw an influx of drunken accidents and incidents that required extra mopping. Her role was to keep the bathrooms spick-and-span at all times. Women would stagger into the bathroom and never see Norma or acknowledge what she was doing—whether she was replacing the hand towels, topping up the soap, or emptying the trash. However, if you did happen to meet eyes with Norma you would be met with the most enormous warm and cheerful smile filled with gratitude.

Remember

EVEN WHEN YOU are in the most unpleasant environment, you can always choose to guide your energy to be cheerful.

Norma was so grateful to have a job that it always made her cheerful. You see, she lived in a tent in downtown Las Vegas for five years. During that time she was assaulted several times, suffered life-threatening pneumonia, experienced ongoing dehydration in the summer heat, lost contact with her children, and never thought that her life would change or that she would become financially stable. Then one day, she applied for a job that she saw in the local newspaper and decided to show up with a cheerful disposition and a willingness to roll up her sleeves and do some hard work. Her newfound sense of purpose was to keep the bathrooms at the Red Rock Casino squeaky clean.

Norma manifested the job, and she was so grateful to have the opportunity to get back on her feet again and also so grateful to be of service to others.

Remember

AS YOU PONDER this story, ask yourself how you can experience a cheerful exchange with someone who you might not take time to pause, see, and appreciate. Please smile and say hello to the person cleaning the bathroom, scanning your groceries, or delivering a package to your doorstep. Your kindness fuels cheerfulness, and it gets passed on.

Dear Universe,

Allow me to be cheerful no matter what I am experiencing in my life. I understand that this energy is contagious and is the common thread that binds us all as human beings. Cheerfulness goes a long way and exhibits the attitude that we are so fortunate to be alive at this point in time.

So be it, so it is.

12 CHERISHED

TO MANIFEST THE energy of feeling cherished in your life, you must cherish others. With my daughter Lulu Dawn, we believe that after suffering five miscarriages in a row to manifest her that it was the same soul trying to get through each time. Every single day, Sean and I say to Lulu: "Thank you for being here." Lulu repeats it back to us, and it's as if there is an unspoken understanding that she is extremely cherished for making the journey to be here, despite the odds.

Remember

FEELING CHERISHED BY your loved ones is so important. You must open your heart and allow space in your life to be made to feel special.

My nana Mollie used to travel from New Zealand to Australia at least once a year to spend time with my sister and me when we were younger. Nana would sit in the middle of the back seat of the car on the way home from the airport. In her late seventies, her hands were so soft and wrinkly, like they had lived a lot of life and cared for a lot of people. She would squeeze my hand and hold on so tight because she was so happy to see us. Just the simple act of holding my grandmother's hand made me feel so cherished. Nana would beam with the happiness of being close to her grandbabies.

Take out your journal and list the ways (no matter how small) you have felt cherished over the course of your life. Now make it your mission to make others feel cherished in the same way to create special memories.

Dear Universe,

I feel so cherished in my life. I am in the process of showing up and manifesting the experience of being cherished for others as well. Thank you for being here with me on this journey and for the awareness that feeling loved is a powerful energy.
So be it, so it is.

---

13 CLEAR

FEELING LIKE YOU'RE in a clear space is so refreshing. Your thoughts flow freely and effortlessly without resistance. You feel grounded within your heart, and you have a clear vision of where your life is headed. You can sense that there is a bigger picture, and you are stepping into a new and vibrant chapter of your life.

To manifest more clarity, it's essential to simplify the amount of information you take into your brain on a daily basis — especially in the first few hours after waking up. Too often people reach for their phone first thing in the morning and mindlessly scroll a social media feed. Try and make it part of your morning ritual to not allow the world in until you have taken care of yourself first. This could be by meditating, drinking water, taking your vitamins, doing stretches or yoga poses — anything that unplugs you from the world to get into a clear space before you begin your day.

Remember

IF YOU CAN see clearly what you wish and desire to manifest into your reality, The Universe will help you create it.

The key element to remember is that clarity will help with harnessing specifically what you want. The Universe or God is always in the details because it can deliver your dreams in direct proportion to your clarity.

Dear Universe,

I now embody the true essence of clarity and inspired action. When I bring more intention to my daily life, I am aware that it helps the energy of possibilities to flow into my reality. I am clear. I trust that my intentions will appear in perfect divine timing.
So be it, so it is.

14 COMPASSIONATE

EVERYONE NEEDS TO practice compassion in their lives as much as possible. In relationships, compassion for what your partner is feeling is the secret to a long-lasting and happy union. We also need to cultivate more self-compassion and stop being so darn hard on ourselves for the silliest little reasons.

Remember

IF YOU CAN hold more compassion in your heart for another person or for yourself beyond the labels of "right" or "wrong," then you are filtering your experience through the eyes of The Universe. It's truly transformative.

I once held the hand of a convicted child sex offender when he was just days away from dying. He couldn't speak at all, so he could only communicate with his eyes. I didn't know the details of what he had done, but I held compassion for the process of dying from a space beyond his inexcusable actions. He had fear in his eyes I will never forget. I showed up in the present moment and held compassion as best I could. Trust me, it was difficult, but it taught me a very valuable lesson.

True compassion cannot be solely reserved for people who you believe deserve it. If you truly believe in the transformative power of compassion, then you trust the energy you put out there will always return to you. Compassion, instead of judgment, is where profound spiritual strength is born.

Dear Universe,

How can I show up with more compassion in this moment? Show me ways to see beyond my judgment to send the energy of love and healing to people in need. This allows me to rise above the energy of wrongness and not contribute to its growth. May my awareness facilitate healing.
So be it, so it is.

---

15 CONFIDENT

IF YOU FEEL confident in who you are and how you present yourself to the world, you are grounded in a beautiful reality of certainty. There are many people out there who would give anything to be more confident and assertive.

Remember

CONFIDENCE CAN BE radiated at different volumes and in different ways, and defined in a multitude of different categories. You are worthy of feeling confident in your own unique way.

I believe that, as long as confidence is paired with a certain sense of humility and compassion for others, it can be projected from a space of authenticity. When people adopt a policy of being "unapologetic" or "shameless" in how they show up in the world, that translates as being self-centered and egocentric. You can be quietly confident and make an incredible difference in the world.

My good friend Scott deMoulin teaches entrepreneurs how to develop their platform speaking skills. I've attended his signature training events and have witnessed firsthand how important it is to be confident. The most fascinating observation for me was that people who I assumed were very confident admitted that they actually experienced nerves. To which Scott taught us this powerful phrase: "If you don't show, they won't know." This means that if you do feel nervous or that your levels of confidence are a little shaky, it probably won't be obvious unless you say something.

The Universe wants you to cultivate confidence, especially in the belief that you are on the right path, right now, and at the right time.

Dear Universe,

Thank you for the boost of confidence in this moment of who
I am and where I am headed in my life. May my energy speak louder than
my words. May I be grounded and exude the essence of inclusion, compassion,
and understanding with everyone I encounter.
So be it, so it is.

---

16 CONNECTED

THERE ARE TWO wonderful ways in which you can feel connected. You can feel the connection between yourself and The Universe — the soulful spark of wonder and magic that reminds you that you are part of everything. Or you can feel connected to the people in your life. Either way is fabulous and ensures that you nurture who you truly are at a soul level.

Feeling connected is how inspiration flows through you to create new ideas, experiences, and adventures for yourself.

Remember

IN ORDER TO feel connected, you must allow the space for connection to unfold in your life.

Friendships are vitally important to develop and nurture a sense of well-being. I'm not talking about just being "social media" friends either. I'm talking about getting away from your screen and sitting down together for a cup of tea or coffee. The new world of social media has actually left so many people feeling isolated, lonely, and disconnected. As humans we need to be surrounded by our people in order to feel energized and empowered.

Take out your journal and write down the names of three people you will connect with this week who you would love to see and haven't made time for in a while. Now meditate on allowing more connection to flow into your current reality . . .

Dear Universe,

Thank you for the wonderful, supportive, funny, smart, beautiful friends and loved ones in my life. I now call forth the energy of limitless possibilities to spark the magic of connection. I am ready for new and exciting adventures, meeting new people, and connecting on an authentic level with as many new kindred spirits as possible.
So be it, so it is.

17 CONTENT

FEELING CONTENT IS one of the best states to occupy within your body, mind, and spirit. To manifest more contentment in your life, you must do things that bring you joy — where your heart is almost bursting with happiness because there is nothing that can make your current reality any better.

Remember

NOT EVERYTHING IN your life has to be perfect in order for you to experience moments of contentment.

You could have over 100 mini-moments of contentment throughout your day, and it all adds up! Try moving through your day and declaring certain situations "mini-moments of contentment." For me it's when I kiss my baby daughter's cheeks in the morning — I am so content in that moment when I connect with Ava. If you need a little help, try and play with The Universe in the following visualization:

Take a moment to imagine that you are sitting in a meditation garden overlooking the ocean. Your legs are crossed, and you are comfortable on the soft grass. The ocean breeze is just the right temperature — not too warm, not too cold. The waves gently break on the shore — lapping on the sand. You hear children laughing in the distance. Everything within your body feels comfortable. You feel at home in your skin. You feel at home in your mind. And you feel at home in your heart, in this moment.

In this pure state of contentment and beingness, you become aware that you don't want anything, or need anything. You're just aware of how relaxed your pace of breathing is and how you feel so blissfully content. You feel a sense of Oneness with the grass you are sitting on. You feel a sense of Oneness with the ocean in front of you. You feel One with the sky, the clouds, and the warmth of the sunshine hitting your skin. This moment is the visual embodiment of feeling content.

Dear Universe,

I am so grateful to be experiencing this level of happiness and contentment right now. Any time I need to recapture the essence of this moment may I ask that you remind me of this feeling in my mind's eye. I am manifesting this experience into my current reality.

So be it, so it is.

18 CREATIVE

BEING CREATIVE IS how the divine essence of The Universe is expressed through you. Creativity raises your vibration, amplifies your energy, and allows beautiful expression to manifest into your life in any way you wish.

Remember

BEING CREATIVE FEEDS your soul on so many levels. It's the best way to spark your connection with The Universe.

Creative energy can manifest through art, writing, music, ideas, cooking, emotional expression, dance, movement, ingenuity . . . and the list goes on.

Find the mode of creativity that is the perfect outlet for who you are at this point in time, and don't be afraid to explore new mediums and methods.

When I was 14, I had an inspired idea that I would design a line of gift-wrap paper and send it around to different manufacturers to see if they would print them. I spent two weeks drawing different kinds of patterns with bright colored markers. I arranged the color copies of the designs into display folders, each with a carefully crafted cover letter. In the letter, I made no mention of my age, but I leveraged my position by mentioning that I had sent the designs to other companies as well.

I had my sights set on Hallmark, but I approached about five companies in total. Hallmark was the biggest company with the most amount of reach. After I sent my proposals out via snail mail, I waited, and waited, and waited . . .

During this time I visualized seeing the finished designs on display racks in department stores and how cool that would feel. I distinctly remember tuning into the feeling. It wasn't about the money, because I didn't even know what the going rate was for designing gift wrap or cards. Anything would have been greatly appreciated, and because I was open to all possibilities the excitement made the experience really fun.

Then one day (after a month or so of waiting), my mother told me there was a woman on the phone for me from Hallmark! They wanted to meet for a discussion to create new products for their spring line. A few months later, I received a check for thousands of dollars for "design services." I felt such a sense of achievement and pride in what my creative energy was able to manifest.

The Universe loves to play with creative energy. Ask for this magnificent energy of possibility to flow through you . . .

Dear Universe,

I open my heart to the flow of pure creative energy to manifest into my reality. May my ideas be drawn and collected from divine sources. Each and every expression of creativity feeds my soul and lights up my heart.
So be it, so it is.

⑲ DEDICATED

IF YOU'RE FEELING dedicated to a project, a mission, a person, or a cause, you are in a wonderful state to manifest something powerful.

Remember

IF IT DOESN'T challenge you, it doesn't change you.

That was the inspirational phrase written in large bold letters on the wall of my daughter Olivia's tae kwon do studio. They not only teach martial arts, but also how to become confident, dedicated young leaders. As a parent, I've sat in the crowd cheering the kids and watching how their dedication and devotion has served them.

Several times I have watched the children being tested for new belt ranks. The instructor holds a board, and they have to kick it so hard that it breaks. If they can't do it, they don't receive their new belts. Some kids try and try and still can't break the board. I can usually see the visible signs of distress: tears welling in their eyes, looking at their parents for reassurance, flushed cheeks, etc. When they finally break the board, there is celebration — the crowd goes wild. If they are unable to break the board, there is a pensive silence. What's so beautiful about this is that the instructor then reminds everyone about the power of dedication and that the belt does not define or represent who they are. It's the dedication to showing up and seeing the lesson for what it is that is the most powerful aspect to remember. So whatever board in your life you are faced with breaking right now — whether it's overcoming an illness, paying off debt, setting boundaries with loved ones, etc. — remember that if you are dedicated to showing up with the right energy to anything you have to face in life, then you are ultimately understanding the lesson.

Dear Universe,

Allow me to show up with dedication and devotion in my life. Show me ways that I can improve as a person. Thank you for the opportunities to grow and thank you for the energy of dedication to remind me that challenges are the key to change. **So be it, so it is.**

20 DELIGHTED

THE ENERGY OF being delighted can manifest in so many beautiful ways. You can feel delighted when you hear some good news, when you receive a gift, when a meal is perfectly satisfying, or when you see a gorgeous bunch of flowers. The world of delight is incredibly important to play in, to help you to feel inspired, and to let The Universe know you are ready and waiting to be delighted more often.

Remember

IF YOU CAN feel truly delighted for the success of someone else, you can spark the possibility of success within yourself.

Some people are unable to feel happy for the success of others, which creates a barrier or a block in the manifestation process. Some people feel jealous, take it personally, feel mean-spirited, and ultimately miss out on the beauty of celebrating the success of others.

Florence Scovel Shinn wrote: "What I wish for you, I wish for myself."

Being delighted is contagious. It's joy in action that is sweeping through the reality and collecting participants in the thrilling party of life.

The Universe loves to see you fully engaged in the essence of delight, which is why it's so important to call it forth into your current reality . . .

Dear Universe,

I am full of delight for what is currently manifesting and what is in the process of manifesting into my reality. Moments of joy are my daily experience and I am so grateful for the opportunity to engage in this vibration. May I find delight in my own success and the success of others.
So be it, so it is.

(21) DEVOTED

WHEN YOU ARE devoted to something, your heart is wide open and your soul feels happy. You are connected to the divine flow of limitless possibilities in your life and you hold deep reverence for the energy that animates everything that has ever existed since the dawn of time.

Devotion isn't just solely reserved for faith and religion. You can be devoted to your family, your work, and causes that you feel passionate about. Spiritual activism is the core component of activating devotion.

Remember

BEING DEVOTED TO something is a deep calling and mission within your soul to be of service for the greater good.

Devotion extends way beyond the ego or self-serving pursuits; it's the celebration of magical miracles and the power of love manifesting into your reality.

You can show your devotion to The Universe through prayer, meditation, service, loving acts, kindness, compassion, using your voice, and holding the awareness that we are all created from the same magical stardust.

> ### Dear Universe,
>
> How can I honor you? How can I serve you? I ask that you show me ways to express my devotion to honoring our sublime connection on the most authentic and pure level. My life is a gift and a blessing, but without devotion to the energy of all-that-is, it becomes meaningless. May reverence be my soulful guiding light to remember where I came from and where I will one day return to.
> **So be it, so it is.**

22 DIVINE

WE ARE ALL divine beings. We might not remember our power all the time, but we are. We are all made of the same magical stardust. To spark the awareness that we are divine is to remind ourselves that we are all connected and part of a bigger picture.

Remember

DIVINE ENERGY IS always flowing through you in the form of inspiration, dreams, wisdom, and curiosity.

This awareness helps you to rise above judgment and remember that we're all together in this great adventure of life. The understanding of this concept also comes with the caveat that nothing is separated from divine energy.

One of my favorite quotes is: Show me where God is not.

The Universe is literally in everything: all things, people, experiences, interactions, emotions, feelings, places, and dreams. It's important to remember that, as part of the wholeness of divine energy, life is happening for us instead of to us.

Dear Universe,

Thank you for the reminder that everything that exists is divine, that there is no separation between me and my judgments. May this awareness spark compassion and understanding within my soul on a level that can help inspire others to remember their own origin of divinity.
So be it, so it is.

 # EAGER

THERE ARE TWO ways you can feel eager. The first is feeling excited anticipation because you're really looking forward to something special happening. The second way is that you are impatient, and all of your energy is obsessed with a specific outcome. One is engaged in the flow of possibility, the other is creating as much resistance as trying to flush a brick down the toilet.

Remember

IF YOU FEEL eager from the space of excitement, you are sending a very clear message to The Universe that you have created the energetic space to manifest your dreams and desires.

Cast your mind back in time for a moment . . .

As a child, did you ever wake up super early on Christmas morning? Perhaps the morning of your birthday? Did you ever have trouble sleeping because you were so darn excited and eager to start your day? This is the magic of feeling eager.

Every single day is an opportunity to expect miracles and engage in the magical feeling of eagerness. However, you must surrender to the feeling because, as the old saying goes, a watched pot never boils.

You must allow the energy of feeling eager to be a jar of fireflies in the pit of your stomach that feels excitement about what The Universe will manifest into your reality very soon.

Dear Universe,

I am now so eager to manifest more magic into my life. I trust that my dreams and desires will appear in perfect divine timing. I feel the powerful spark of childlike excitement for what is in the process of being created and delivered into my reality.
So be it, so it is.

㉔ ELATED

THERE IS NOTHING sweeter than feeling elation. There's this magical excitement that unfolds when you feel so ecstatically happy about your experience.

Elation usually manifests when special events unfold in our lives — when you get engaged, when you beat a personal best, when you stare into your newborn baby's eyes for the first time, or even when you win an eBay auction for something you really wanted.

Remember

ELATION IS THE essence of joy, and you must manifest it into your reality as often as you can.

On my 33rd birthday, I was blindfolded and taken to a secret location where a pink limousine was waiting for me. Sean had arranged for my family and friends to ride with us to the city (we were living outside Melbourne, Australia, at the time). When we got out of the limo, Sean started singing with some street buskers — who I later discovered he had rehearsed with. He then got down on one knee and asked me to marry him. There were at least a hundred strangers watching the very public proposal, to which I said, with as much elation in my voice as possible, "Yes!"

I felt like I was on cloud nine — I was so ecstatically happy. You see, elation resides in the magical moments of life like this.

How can you manifest more joy? What are some ways you have experienced feeling elated over the years? How can you relive it?

Dear Universe,

Show me ways that I can experience more elation in my daily life. In my times of feeling a little down or depressed may I remember special memories and moments that brought me extreme happiness. Allow me to spark the energy of elation in my heart.
So be it, so it is.

---

25 EMPOWERED

IT IS CRUCIAL to feel empowered in your life — because it's your life and because YOU matter. Parents must become experts in the field of empowering their children to make good, healthy, and smart choices for themselves.

Remember

WHEN YOU FEEL empowered, you have the power to change the world. Helping humanity grow and heal is how everyone on the planet gets the opportunity to become empowered.

Your voice is closely linked to your levels of empowerment — how you choose to use your power, the causes that you support, and your interest in spiritual activism. For years I kept my mouth shut, kept creative ideas to myself, and kept my thoughts silent. I didn't realize how powerful I actually was when I decided to create my own business and share it with others. Being an entrepreneur was ultimately the identity I adopted that empowered me to leave ten years of domestic violence.

Back then I would never have thought that sharing my oh-so-personal experiences would help empower millions of people around the world to claim their own path of magnificence. You see, empowered people empower people. When you can identify that you have a responsibility to be a custodian of consciousness the world becomes a sweet place to reside.

The Universe always holds the awareness that you are empowered in every sense of the word when you are ready to step forward into your heart space and shine.

Dear Universe,

Thank you for the reminder of my power. Thank you for the clarity of my vision. Thank you for guiding me to connect with the right people in order to be inspired. May I lead with love and encapsulate the soul of leadership on every conceivable level.
So be it, so it is.

26 ENERGIZED

WHEN YOU ARE full of energy, you are living life to the fullest and you remember that you are capable of anything your heart desires. This is ultimately how The Universe always wants you to feel — energized! When you feel energized, you can follow the paths of intuition, of inspiration, of creativity, and of transformation.

Remember

IF YOU DON'T make it a goal to live a life of amplified energy, you are missing out on the magic of being human.

Have you ever heard someone declare to The Universe that they have no energy, low energy, or that they feel tired all the time? Guess what? There are so many wonderful things that can be done to remedy the situation and feel energized again.

You must do the following five things that will help to get the energy flowing through your body and your soul:

1. Move your body because it creates energy (dance, walk, run, just move!).
2. Nourish your body (eat healthy and vibrant food).
3. Water your body (hydration helps with energy levels).
4. Rest your body (an overworked body will burn out).
5. Honor your body (listen to the clues and messages from your body — it's telling you what it needs).

The energy will always flow when you take care of yourself, instead of draining all of your energetic resources with habits that don't serve you. Meditation is also an excellent way to ask The Universe to amplify your energy levels . . .

Dear Universe,

I am a conduit for the flow of infinite energy. I have an endless supply
of energy to tap into to create magic in every area of my life. May I honor my
body and nurture my entire being so that I can be of service for my passion
and purpose in the world.
So be it, so it is.

㉗ ENLIGHTENED

I BELIEVE THAT enlightenment and the interpretation of the manifestation of enlightenment is very subjective. No one truly knows for sure what it means or entails to be an "enlightened being." I do believe, however, that people can indeed get glimpses of feeling enlightened. The manifestation of peace in the present moment and the understanding of divine love is probably the closest definition that my human mind can comprehend.

Remember

THE GOAL OF life is not necessarily to obtain enlightenment. It's to enjoy this wild adventure called "life" and to grow from the obstacles and detours we are presented with.

I believe we chose to be on this earth to learn. It's a sacred contract that almost helps us to make sense of the times in our lives that are painful or difficult.

In Buddhism, enlightenment is defined as a final blessed state marked by the absence of desire or suffering. In my opinion, both desire and suffering are where the beauty and fullness of life can flow through you. There is nothing (and I mean no thing) that is untouched by the presence of The Universe. Every event, person, place, and experience manifests into your life for a beautiful and powerful reason.

Dear Universe,

In this moment, I seek peace and presence. May enlightenment manifest
in such a way that I am able to understand life from a wide range of vantage points
and perspectives. May my heart and mind operate from a unified
paradigm, and may any judgment remind me that the beautiful energy of
creation flows through and animates all that is.
So be it, so it is.

100 MINI-MEDITATIONS TO EMBRACE LOVE

28 ENTHUSIASTIC

KIDS ARE SO enthusiastic, it's powerful. Tiny events in life become oh-so-exciting: everything from jumping up and down when you find out there are cookies, to saying "wow!" with your eyes wide open when you see someone's house decorated in sparkly lights for the holidays.

Remember

THE MORE ENTHUSIASM you can express for your life, the more The Universe will show up and deliver experiences to express awe and wonder.

My parents always remind me of how enthusiastic I was as a child. When I was nine years old, our third grade musical was a watered-down version of Andrew Lloyd Webber's *Cats*. Our costumes were very low key. All-black leotards, eyeliner for drawing a nose and whiskers, paper ears, and pantyhose stuffed with newspaper for our tails. The opening number was a group of about 20 of us. The music started, and the legs started moving in unison — except for mine. I felt so much enthusiasm for the performance and for being seen by my parents that 19 cats went one way, and Sarah Prout went the other way with a bunch of rogue, unchoreographed moves. It was the epitome of enthusiasm that literally made me stand out (or dance out) from the crowd.

So how can you replicate the magic of enthusiasm in your own life right now? What can you allow yourself to get super-excited about?

Dear Universe,

Show me creative ways my soul can merge into the powerful energy of enthusiasm. May I feel the giddy spark of excitement in my heart that all good things are manifesting into my life. May I allow myself to fully express this wonder in any way that it needs to.
So be it, so it is.

29 EXPANSIVE

WHEN YOU'RE READY to begin the next chapter of your life, you just know it. There's a feeling of expansion within your heart that you are finally ready to take a leap of faith or perhaps spread your wings and fly.

I had such an intuitive nudge within my soul when I was finally ready to leave Australia to move to America. I had no clue how the move would be possible. I'd just given birth to my daughter Lulu, and our business wasn't doing very well. We also had concerns of whether or not Max (my first husband) would sign papers to allow my older children to leave the country permanently. In the end, The Universe unraveled all of the details in the perfect way, at the perfect time. I just had to trust in the process along the way.

Remember

THE CALL WITHIN your heart to expand your life can sometimes be scary and uncertain. However, it's usually based on your soul's desire for growth and transformation. Trust your intuition; it's leading you to a new chapter in your life.

As humans, The Universe designed us to be ever-expanding beings in the nature of our consciousness. The aim of the game is to expand and to flourish, which is why it's so important that you don't hold yourself back from adventure and new experiences.

Your main objective on this journey is to say yes to the idea of expansion. Whether you move to a different country, travel, accept a new job, or say yes to a blind date — The Universe will always reward you for your willingness to view life from an expansive perspective.

Dear Universe,

Open my heart and my mind to new and exciting
experiences and adventures. I trust that you will guide me to
intuitively follow the right path of inspired action to take.
So be it, so it is.

---

30 EXPRESSIVE

YOU CAN NEVER feel or be too expressive. How you express yourself is entirely up to you, with the caveat to be sure that it doesn't hurt anyone else in the process. How your expression manifests in your life could be a wonderful world of creative possibilities from art, to music, fashion, spoken word, poetry, dance, cooking, or writing — the outlets are endless!

Remember

LEARNING HOW TO express yourself is imperative to making sure that your needs are met by the people in your life who you love you. It's a vital way to process the full spectrum of emotions that you experience on your journey and to document them.

Many of us have perfected the art form of expressing ourselves from a negative vantage point. And some of us don't truly recognize the avenues that would ultimately serve us the best in terms of authentic and heartfelt expression. It surely is a gift to be able to make yourself feel understood and to know that your ideas are expressed in a way that makes you feel valued, heard, and seen.

But here's an example of when being expressive goes rogue and a little haywire:

One day Sean and I were having an argument. I had stormed into his office demanding his attention, and because I wasn't able to express myself in a way that created a safe space, Sean decided to shut down the conversation and told me he didn't wish to speak anymore. He had a giant jar of jelly beans on his desk. As a guess, I'd say there were well over 700 jelly beans in the jar. I felt the overwhelming urge to continue to express myself and proceeded to tip all of the jelly beans out onto the floor. It was like a rainbow confetti cannon had spontaneously entered the room! My overly expressive action caused instant silence and weirdness. I definitely regretted that action, but it became a lesson in inappropriate expression, that's for sure!

The point here is to allow and create mutual space within your relationships, friendships, and partnerships that creates boundaries for when you need to express yourself and when you need to allow the clear space to manifest to do so. Nurture yourself creatively as much as possible. Buy some paints or a sketchbook, discover new music, learn an instrument, buy a jar of jelly beans, learn a different language — the possibilities are endless and only limited by your imagination.

Dear Universe,

Show me the best way to express how I feel in the most appropriate way that energizes my energy and sparks the essence of joy in my soul. May I find curiosity in discovering new and wonderful ways to express how I feel in each moment.
So be it, so it is.

31 FESTIVE

ONE OF MANY aspects I adore about living in the United States is how the American people celebrate various occasions throughout the year. There seem to be so many more holidays than I remember celebrating in Australia. For instance, I love how in stores the seasons are celebrated, like the large images of flowers and sunshine in the spring, and the pumpkin spice and Halloween merchandise in the fall. There is an excitement behind the energy of engaging in festivities. It's actually the key ingredient in the process of manifestation. It's joy! Being festive activates and encapsulates joy, abundance, community, and connection.

For many years, I would sit on the sidelines of my own life and not fully allow myself to enjoy special days (holidays = holy days) such as Christmas or Easter. Now I love them! All of them! They are so entwined with the beauty of tradition and honoring the generations before us, those who got us to where we are today.

Remember

YOU CAN CREATE your own holidays, traditions, and festivities in your life.

The more you do this, the more it sends a signal out to The Universe that you are engaged in playfulness, levity, and joy. If you're tuned in to the magic of feeling festive, or you have the intention to, The Universe is always willing to show up and be the life of your party . . .

Dear Universe,

Feeling festive is my way of expressing joy. May I be the bearer of happiness, of fun, and of laughter. May we celebrate and party like it's 1999 because life is sweeter when you find a reason to honor the beauty of being alive.
So be it, so it is.

---

32 FIERCE

FEELING FIERCE? PERHAPS you see yourself as a badass right now, and you're dishing out karma to the people who deserve it, as if you are a spiritual vigilante seeking to return the world to a state of justice.

Feeling fierce has its place, as long as there is some space for softness and compassion too. This is an important difference to make. For instance, if you mess with or bully my kids, I will radically transform into a mama bear right before your eyes. I'll do anything within my power to protect my babies — or anyone's babies for that matter.

Being fierce, however, does not need to be only in a conflict resolution situation. You can be fierce and fearless when you are negotiating a contract, when you are dressing for a cocktail party, when you are marching to support a cause you are passionate about — the fierce list of possibilities are endless!

Remember

BEING FIERCE DOESN'T mean being scary; it can simply mean that you are emphatic and fair. You're on a mission to create impactful change.

Dear Universe,

Draw forth the strength to be fearless and fierce in the times that require me to protect my loved ones. May I choose my battles wisely and approach them with a sense of compassion and strength. May I always be aware of the danger of assumptions. May the fierce energy of empowerment flow through me as it is needed.
So be it, so it is.

---

33 FLOWING

TO BE IN a state of what is known as "flow" is to be fully immersed in energized focus. It's when you could do a certain activity all day, losing the concept of time and space. This is how we identify our passions and what we love to do. When you feel as if you are flowing, a whole new world of creative and wondrous possibilities begins to emerge.

Remember

LEARNING HOW TO get in a flow state is vital to moving your life forward.

You can do this through meditation, setting powerful intentions, and also stepping out of your usual routine in order to gather your thoughts.

When you're truly in flow, you feel uplifted and motivated to take inspired action. The Universe loves you in this state because once you build that momentum, signs of alignment in your life will be delivered.

You'll meet new people who will help you on your path. You'll also attract the right resources and events that will unfold the next set of steps for you. The best thing you can do is say "yes" to new opportunities and adventures that life presents. You'll notice that the more in flow you get with this stuff, the more amazing "miracles" will unfold and give you "proof" (not that you need it) that The Universe is always ready and waiting to play with you.

Dear Universe,

My heart and my mind are open to the flow of infinite wisdom and possibilities. Guide me to experience and attract new opportunities, new friends, new places to visit, and new creative endeavors. Motivation is sparked within my heart when I am in a state of flow. Life is effortless, energized, fun, and free.
So be it, so it is.

34 FOCUSED

THERE ARE MANY times in our lives that require us to engage in the energy of focus. Whether you're studying for an exam, about to take your driver's license test, or playing a game of Operation and have to pay close attention so the buzzer doesn't go off, that's when focus is your friend. However, as a society we are all experiencing shorter and shorter attention spans. Multitasking when you need to focus is actually really bad for your brain. If you're trying to write an essay for your psychology assignment and you're listening to Spotify and intermittently scrolling through your Instagram feed, then focus is truly not possible.

Remember

WHERE YOUR ATTENTION goes your energy flows.

What are you focused on? Where is your focus most of the time? Are you able to sit in the presence of a task, or is it tricky for you to sit still and absorb the information? If you can refine the art of focus, you can create and build something meaningful.

If you do have trouble focusing, stay away from stimulants such as sugar and coffee, or sugar in coffee. Also connect to The Universe and ask for the support and guidance you require to stay on track and channel your energy in a streamlined manner . . .

Dear Universe,

May I now embody the core foundation of focus. May the task that I need to complete be done in a manner that amplifies my ability to focus clearly on what I want to achieve. May I always keep my eyes on the prize.
So be it, so it is.

35 FORGIVING

FORGIVENESS WILL SET your soul free. Holding on to the energy of the past will stop you from creating a beautiful and exciting future for yourself. When you can get to an authentic space where you feel a true sense of forgiveness, your life will radically and magically transform.

Remember

FORGIVENESS IS A choice. It doesn't mean you forget, it just means that you let go of the energy that binds you to the person or the experience.

For instance, I 100 percent completely forgive my first husband, Max, for our ten years of domestic violence and shared pain. I have literally zero interest in holding on to the past. The only reason I have shared my experience throughout this book (and my teachings over the years) is to show that I'm a survivor who is capable of forgiving and setting myself free. In fact, I am so grateful to Max for our experience together. I've often said that I wouldn't change anything, even if I could. The buckets of tears, the loneliness, the bruises, the neglect — I would not change a single thing because of the soulful transaction of consciousness that unfolded. My story has helped others to find safety, meaning, and purpose. I would gladly go through another ten years of sadness if I knew what was waiting for me on the other side. It's the beauty of life in her full radiance when you can forgive and see the purpose in the pain. I love Max on a soul level — he knows that, and I honor him for his role in my life's mission. He's on his path, and I'm on mine. There is no shame, no resentment, and no heavy grudge to hold — just the intention to trust in The Universe for the lesson.

Keep in mind it's not a simple path to forgive. It took me many years to finally dismantle the energetic hold on my soul. However, as cheesy as it sounds, time is a healer. Set the intention to free yourself from the pain of the past and The Universe is ready and waiting to hold your hand and remind you that in time it will all make sense and be okay . . .

Dear Universe,

I forgive (insert name here) for (insert reason here). Most important I also show myself forgiveness. I release the energy of the past and move forward into a bright, happy, vibrant future where I am creating special memories with my friends and loved ones. Life is too short to hold on to grudges. I let the situation go with love, light, and compassion.
So be it, so it is.

36 FREE

THERE IS NOTHING more important than feeling free. Having a sense of freedom in your life is the sweetest nectar for your soul.

I remember when I finally left ten years of domestic violence behind me. For the first time in my adult life, I was living in my own apartment, paying my own bills, managing my own money, and raising the kids in a way that I wanted to. There was no oppression. I was no longer afraid. I was free, finally free.

My apartment was old. There was no heating or air-conditioning. I didn't own a fridge or a washing machine, so I would scrub the clothes in the bathtub by hand. For the first time in my grown-up life — at the age of 30 — I was able to make my own decisions. I was living on less than $15 per day most days, but even without much money, I felt like I was the wealthiest person in the world.

Remember

HAVING SOVEREIGNTY IN your life is the essence of experiencing feeling free.

In your mind's eye, imagine that you are a bird flying in the sky. You are soaring above the people, the trees, the trivialities of daily life. Capture this essence of freedom as a snapshot that you can visit during your meditations . . .

Dear Universe,

My body, my mind, and my spirit is free. This beautiful freedom manifests in various ways throughout my life. Freedom allows me to live life in its full expression of beauty. I am so thankful to release the burdens of the past and step into a future of free-spirited adventure.
So be it, so it is.

37 GENEROUS

THE BUDDHA SAID that no true spiritual life is possible without a generous heart. Generosity aligns itself with an inner feeling of abundance — the feeling that we have enough to share and enough to give.

The feeling of being generous is a heartwarming experience. It means you are showing up and being of service to others in the world.

One person who I believe embodies the energy of true generosity is my mother-in-law, Lauren. When I married Sean (her son), she embraced my two older children (Thomas and Olivia) as her own grandchildren. In 2014, she was diagnosed with breast cancer and continued to be the kind and generous spirit she had always been. In fact, her life is devoted to helping other people face the same scary levels of uncertainty that she faced. Now her weeks are filled with helping to raise awareness for breast cancer patients and survivors like herself. She delivers Christmas trees to people who can't afford to celebrate the holidays, helps with charity drives, marches for women's rights, and remembers each and every one of her seven grandchildren's birthdays.

Remember

IF YOU HAVE a generous heart, you will live an empowered life filled with meaning and purpose.

Spend time observing others who are generous — and not just with their money. Spend time watching others who are generous with their listening skills, empathy, and levels of presence, and be inspired to be more generous with your own listening skills, empathy, and presence.

Dear Universe,

May I activate the essence of generosity in every area of my life.
I remember that being generous with my heart will attract more abundance
or me to be able to support more people in need.
So be it, so it is.

38 GENTLE

MY MOTHER TELLS the story of giving birth to me and trying to lose her baby weight extraordinarily quickly. She said she didn't eat much and would smoke like a chimney. She would run for several hours per day, until she ended up having a slight stroke from the excessive exercise. The time following a woman giving birth should be gentle. None of this crazy punishing nonsense my mother was engaging in!

The lack of gentleness on herself had a ripple effect on me. I remember just four weeks after I gave birth to my son, Thomas, I was sitting cross-legged on the floor and noticed for the first time that I had cellulite on my thighs. This is when my inner thoughts became anything but gentle and began to attack my sense of self.

Remember

YOU MUST BE gentle with yourself and stop believing that you are not enough.

When you want to manifest more gentleness in your life, spend some time around babies — any baby. Whether you have kids of your own or if you want to visit a baby panda at the zoo or a fresh batch of baby ducklings, notice how you always show up with the energy of gentleness, and then treat yourself with the same energy. It's important that you learn to do so. Self-compassion and gentleness are key components in your self-care toolbox.

Dear Universe,

May I be gentle with myself and create a cease-fire in my mind, where my thoughts no longer have the power to dictate how they think I should be. I am enough. I am kind. I am gentle with others and with myself. My words are chosen from the space of empowerment.
So be it, so it is.

39 GRACEFUL

BEING GRACEFUL IS about more than just making sure that you don't burp in public, slump your shoulders, or have a ketchup stain on your chin. It's not only the way you carry your body, but how you maintain awareness about your actions as well as the thoughts and energy that you exude out there into the world. People who are graceful are naturally elegant and hold a magnetizing energy that others seem drawn to.

Remember

BEING GRACEFUL IS the embodiment of grace. Literally being full of grace. And as you know, grace is the divine energy that is the constant reminder that The Universe is flowing through us.

One of the first steps to feeling graceful is to pause before you react to things, people, places, or events. Develop a filter of considered thought where you build a buffer before you blurt out your initial knee-jerk reaction. Being graceful is slowing down to consider a situation and how you can approach it from the vantage point of conscious awareness.

The Universe will always hear your request to embody the essence of grace.

Dear Universe,

I now embody the energy of gracefulness. I lean into conscious leadership and the responsibility that how I behave in the world is a reflection of the divine, all-pervading living energy that flows through all that is.
So be it, so it is.

# 40 GRACIOUS

AFTER 29 YEARS of marriage, Mary slept with her much younger next-door neighbor, Keith. Mary's husband, Antonio, felt as if the situation was being rubbed in his face. Over the fence, he could see the new couple flaunting their affection. And then, one day, Mary left them both and moved to another state. Antonio felt the deep pain of betrayal and Keith felt used. The two men didn't know one another.

A few weeks after Mary left, there was a knock at Antonio's door. It was Keith, stating that the hot water in his house wasn't working, and wanted to see if his neighbors had the same problem.

"You can use the hot water here if you need to. It's still working fine," offered Antonio.

Now, this story might not seem like a big deal, but the point here is to illustrate how the opportunity to be gracious can arise in the weirdest situations.

Remember

THE MORE YOU rise above judgment and past hurt and hostility, the more gracious you can be when it comes to being kind — even if it's to a stranger who slept with your wife.

The Universe can work through you when you are open to being gracious . . .

Dear Universe,

How may I be of service today?
How can I help inspire others through your divine grace?
So be it, so it is.

41 GRATEFUL

ARE YOU A glass half empty or a glass half full kind of person? Or maybe you fluctuate between the two. Does every cloud have a silver lining? Having an "attitude of gratitude" in your life is a deep spiritual practice that can transform most, if not all situations.

Remember

YOUR PERCEPTION ULTIMATELY shapes your reality.

The Universe will deliver more things for you to be grateful for if you weave appreciation into your daily spiritual practice. Taking time to write down three things that you are grateful for on a daily basis will radically help to improve the levels of happiness you experience in your life.

If you are already feeling as if you occupy a space of gratitude right now, please make sure that you capture it on paper! Try it for a week in your journal and also note how it has made you feel.

Taking inventory of your levels of appreciation is so good for relationships, your bank account, and also how you feel about yourself. The Universe loves it when you are in an attitude of gratitude.

Dear Universe,

I am so grateful for everything in my life. I am so grateful
for my connection with you. I understand that holding the feeling of
appreciation in my heart for anything that appears in my reality is
how I show trust that you are looking out for me. May I always remember
the power of saying thank you. May I always express appreciation for
people who help me. May I show gratitude to the loved ones in my life.
So be it, so it is.

---

42 GROUNDED

LIFE WILL TAKE you on many wondrous and magical adventures. You'll experience the highest of highs and the lowest of lows because that's all part of the exciting journey. However, an important element that is often overlooked is the process of remaining grounded — feeling that your feet are firmly planted on the ground and you are centered. Sometimes you might get "carried away with the fairies" or "have your head stuck in the clouds." It's definitely fun to allow yourself to get swept up in the magic. Just keep in mind a grounded sense of reality — especially when you're on a manifesting journey to intentionally create your own reality.

Remember

BEING GROUNDED WILL help you make decisions from a space of openness, willingness, and transformation.

If your energy is allowed to run wild, and you're not taking time to be in your body and feel centered and calm, then all hell could break loose. The higher you climb, the further you'll fall. Grounding is imperative to managing your energy efficiently.

There are many creative and powerful ways to ground yourself. You could try yoga, breathing exercises, eating a nutritious meal, meditation, or standing barefoot on a lawn or sand (this process is called "Earthing"). Tune in to ask yourself what will help you be grounded in the present moment and not let your energy get carried away and spiral out of control.

Dear Universe,

May I be grounded in the gift of this present moment. I am aware of the energy contained within my body and seek balance and harmony to guide an inspired path forward.
So be it, so it is.

43 GUIDED

WHEN YOU FEEL guided and silently supported by The Universe, life becomes a wild and fun adventure. Receiving guidance in the form of intuition, dreams, wisdom, or advice from a trusted friend or mentor is incredibly important. As long as you remember that you have the power to choose your path and that no one else can tell you what to do; they can just give you gentle guidance to make your own decisions. Guidance is yours and yours alone to attach meaning to.

Remember

WHEN YOU SEEK alignment with an open heart, The Universe will respond by sending "divine winks" that you are on the right path.

It's also helpful to take into consideration the asking process. If you wish to receive signs of alignment and guidance from The Universe, you need to ask. Put the intention out there into the world and watch your reality reflect back to you messages from your higher self and the cosmos.

Take out your journal and make a list of the signs that you are collecting from The Universe. A sign could be a number, roses, rainbows, a specific song, butterflies, a symbol — whatever means something specifically to you and has significance. Record how you feel about each sign and make sure you note the date.

When you feel guided, you ultimately learn to trust that everything is unfolding exactly as it is meant to.

Dear Universe,

I am open to receiving guidance and wisdom. I am ready to allow signs of alignment to flow into my life to remind me that I am on the right path of inspired action.
So be it, so it is.

44 HAPPY

IF YOU DESIRE to manifest happiness into your current reality, it is simply a choice in this very moment. Happiness is not a future destination, and it's 100 percent up to you to create happiness for yourself.

Remember

YOU'RE NOT GOING to be happy when you lose the weight, when you meet your soulmate, or when you manifest a million dollars. Be happy now. The JOY is in the journey.

Too often people make others responsible for how they feel. They make others responsible for their happiness. Thoughts such as you should make me happy or you don't make me happy are silly because they shift responsibility into the hands of someone who does not and should not hold that kind of power over you. Take your power back!

Your role is to lean in to the things that bring you joy — wherever they are. This is where true happiness resides, when you can surround yourself with the people, places, and experiences that light you up from the inside.

Call forth the magic of The Universe to help you spark happiness from deep inside your soul . . .

Dear Universe,

Thank you for this moment of happiness. I am aware of the ability to guide my energy back to a state of joy and appreciation whenever I feel called to do so. I now release others from the burden of being responsible for how I feel and I take my own power back to seek happiness in each and every delicious moment of life.
So be it, so it is.

45 HEALED

WE ARE ALL born with the power to heal ourselves—both emotionally and physically. Your body was created by The Universe in such a way to maintain a sense of well-being and balance. Healing is your natural state—where you are regenerating and creating billions of new cells in each and every moment. Healing involves rising above limiting beliefs and holding the awareness that anything is possible. It's a sacred mission when you are seeking to be healed. For many, it can be a powerful spiritual quest to know themselves on a deeper level.

Remember

IF YOU ARE unwell, it's a call to step into your power and remember to choose the path of wellness with your thoughts, feelings, and actions.

In order to feel healed, you must tune in to the power of your heart, use affirmations that empower you, and surround yourself with the support that you need in order to thrive.

Visualization is also an incredibly powerful tool in the healing process:

Close your eyes for a moment and imagine that you are surrounded in vibrant rose-gold light. This light is entering into your mind and healing your emotions. This light is entering into your body and healing your organs, your cells, your blood, and your bones. This light is infusing itself into your heart and permeating your entire being with the energy of vibrant health and wellness. See this visualization in your mind's eye on a daily basis and watch how you begin to feel.

Dear Universe,

I am so incredibly grateful for the health and wellness that I experience in my reality. Thank you for healing me in body, in mind, and in spirit. I am empowered to make the right choices with the thoughts I think, the words I speak, the feelings I feel, and the nourishment that I allow into my body.
So be it, so it is.

 **HELPFUL**

FEELING HELPFUL IS engaging in the essence of service. This is a powerful element in the manifestation process. Constantly asking yourself how you can be more helpful is a way to spark more joy in your life and the lives of others.

Remember

BEING HELPFUL COMES from having a kind heart. The world needs as many kindhearted people as possible right now.

Opening the door for someone is a helpful act of kindness. When someone asks for directions, it is an opportunity to be helpful. Alternatively, if you see someone in need and you reach out to offer assistance, it can mean so much to someone in their time of crisis. Feeling like you're actually doing something important and making a difference in the world can be a wonderful way to strengthen your sense of self and purpose.

Helpful people show up in a moment of need no matter what. The first responders on the scene of a mass shooting or natural disaster are true angels and heroes within our society. They roll up their sleeves and serve, despite the danger. It's because they remember that we're all in this together and that we should always treat others in the way we wish to be treated.

I once witnessed an old lady collapse in the supermarket. There were six people around her. Three stepped forward and fell to their knees to offer assistance. Three stepped aside and quickly walked away. I placed my hand on her shoulder and asked if she was okay.

"Yes, dear. Thank you," she said.

It doesn't take much to feel helpful, but when you do, it feels great — like you are connecting to what's important in life and doing your best.

Dear Universe,

Reveal to me ways that I can be more helpful with my friends, loved ones, and total strangers. Allow me to be of service and show me ways that I can offer kindness to people in need.
So be it, so it is.

47 HONEST

THERE IS NOTHING more important to your moral compass than embracing honesty. If you can know and trust with every fiber of your being that you are truthful and integrity driven, then you will be able to sleep well at night. People who tell fibs or shamelessly bend the truth to suit themselves only create pain on their journey through life.

Remember

USE YOUR WORDS wisely. The energy of false information, accusations, and dishonest behavior will always return to you with astounding accuracy.

One thing I teach my Manifesting Academy students is not to start or finish a sentence with "to be honest with you . . ." As an example: "To be honest with you, I never really liked her rhubarb crumble anyway."

This presupposes that everything you have just said, or are about to say, isn't the truth.

I have taught my children that if they find anything greater than a penny on the road or in the supermarket, to either donate it or to give it to the cashier. I once saw my son spot a five-dollar bill on the ground. There was a moment where he hesitated and I told him to hand it to the guy bagging the groceries. Sure enough, the guy was so impressed by his sense of honesty that he told Thomas to keep the money. What goes around comes around! It was a valuable lesson that honesty is rewarded by The Universe.

In order to manifest the incredible energy of being committed to being honest, you must make a lifelong commitment and declare an affirmation to The Universe that goes a little something like this:

Dear Universe,

Give me strength to be honest and up-front when truth is required. Give me the ability to show compassion for others when they are out of integrity. May I lead with love, may my levels of honesty inspire others to seek a similar path.
So be it, so it is.

48 HOPEFUL

THERE IS SOME serious magic behind the energy of feeling hopeful. It means that you're optimistic, you're positive, and you're eager that your intention will soon manifest in the way that you wish it would. In fact, The Universe wants you to be in this state to make it easier for your desires to appear in your reality.

Remember

FEELING HOPEFUL IS the best space to occupy in your life. It's sending The Universe a very clear message that you are ready to receive your desired outcomes.

If I think back to the times in my life that I felt hopeful, they cover such a broad spectrum of experiences. I was hopeful every time I took a pregnancy test. Those moments are so exciting. All signs point to being pregnant, but the pee-stick test is the final confirmation. I've been hopeful when I sent out various book proposals over the years. I've been hopeful that change would happen, that loved ones would get better, and that something (anything) would disrupt the status quo.

Hopefulness is a lightness in your heart that holds the intention that everything will work out for the best and for the greatest good.

Dear Universe,

I now embody the energy and the essence of hopefulness that everything will work out perfectly as it should. I trust in divine timing and understand that my intentions will manifest in direct proportion to the hopefulness that I hold in in my heart. May I always meet situations with hope, instead of doubt.
So be it, so it is.

---

49 INFINITE

YOU ARE AN infinite being. We are all part of the same fabric of Oneness. To give you an example:

After my daughter Lulu was born via C-section, the doctor was about to begin stitching me up. The anesthetic started to wear off, which meant I was able to feel everything. I could feel the air on my open abdomen; it was agony.

"I can feel that! I can feel that!" I began to say in a mad panic.

The scene turned from a miracle into a horror movie within minutes.

The last thing I remember was drifting and not feeling like I was asleep, but being aware that I was somewhere else, up high, above everything and part of everything, almost like on another level of the hospital where I could see everything that was going on at once.

The pain left me. I could see the color pink everywhere. I was in a large corridor that had rooms and doors, just like the hospital, but different. Behind each door I could simultaneously see different scenes. I could see and feel Sean sitting with Lulu, I could see my body being stitched up, I could see the nurses, I could see Thomas and Olivia, I felt as if I was one with Lulu, and I was peering out into the world from her new perspective. It was like I was flying around this corridor, this weird realm, and not sure how to get back to myself, to my consciousness. I felt infinite.

Suddenly I realized I had no control over waking up and it became a little scary. I loved this place I was in. It felt peaceful. But the more at peace I felt, the more the memory of who I was and what my purpose was started to fade.

I distinctly remember asking myself: "Am I dead? Who am I?"

I didn't remember who I was. Then I heard a voice say the names of my children. The voice wasn't mine, and it wasn't clear. It was like an anchor of love to return me to who I was. At 7:11 p.m. I woke up back in my body after a crazy adventure into the infinite.

Remember

WE LIVE IN a world of infinite possibilities and the world beyond is the purest essence of infinite unconditional love. We are so much more than our physical reality.

Dear Universe,

Guide me to remember that my true nature is infinite. May I feel the expansive and all-pervading divine energy within my heart. May love be my channel for connecting within the world.
So be it, so it is.

50 INQUISITIVE

"There are many answers you have received, but not yet heard."
— HELEN SCHUCMAN, *A COURSE IN MIRACLES*

MANY PEOPLE THINK they can show their intelligence by providing and knowing the answers all the time. Incredibly aware and smart people know that people can truly assess your level of cleverness by the questions you ask. The soulful key is to make sure the questions you ask are truly inquisitive and come from a space of curiosity.

Remember

ASK QUESTIONS. Ask a lot of questions, and always be inquisitive about the nature of reality. It's how your consciousness will expand.

Some people don't like to ask questions if they don't understand something. They fear that it could make them appear like they are not as smart as they'd like to present themselves to be. Asking questions is how you grow.

It's an invitation to grow when you have a soul-load of questions that need answering. Just understand that some of the answers you might hear on one level might not ring true until the right time.

The Universe loves an inquisitive soul. It's fun to play with.

Dear Universe,

Reveal to me the answers to my most burning questions. Remind me of the power to ask questions and to get curious about the information I am seeking. Also remind me to explore different sources of information and to be truly objective about the information I am presented with. There are many methods and many ways.
So be it, so it is.

(51) INSPIRED

THE ENERGY OF feeling inspired is so miraculous. It's the energy of potential, of creativity, and of joy. You're on a wondrous journey into the realm where dreams meet intuition and anything is possible.

Inspiration works really well with something known as the "flow state." It's a state of meditation — of mindfulness — that you experience while taking inspired action and feeling as if The Universe is working through you.

Remember

WHEN YOU FEEL inspired, you are manifesting miracles, and The Universe is orchestrating all of the divine details to support you on your adventure.

Incredible ideas can often be birthed when you are feeling inspired and connected to The Universe. The story is that Paul McCartney came up with the melody for the Beatles' "Yesterday" — the most-covered song in music history — from a dream he had one night in 1964.

Artists source their inspiration from nature, observation, experience, and intuition. Writers also draw from the subject matter they find the most fascinating. When you have sparked the energy of inspiration within your soul, you are living life intentionally. You are a powerful creator painting the masterpiece that is your own reality.

Always play with The Universe to call forth and invoke the essence of inspiration when you need it . . .

Dear Universe,

I now flow with inspired ideas to create something beautiful, magical, and meaningful in my life. May my mind be given a series of actions that will help to support me on this path of inspiration. May I be guided, may I be uplifted, may I feel inspired.
So be it, so it is.

52 INTUITIVE

WE'VE ALL FELT that "knowing" in the pit of our stomachs, when something just doesn't feel right. On the flip side of this, you might have felt the full force of alignment and a big giant "YES" when something does feel right. The key point to remember is to hone and honor your intuitive faculties. Allowing your heart to be guided by what you feel intuitively will strengthen that muscle and make it more accurate when you need it most.

Remember

WHEN YOU DESIRE to manifest higher levels of intuition in your life, ask The Universe to support you.

An extremely underutilized intuitive resource is tapping into the power of our dreams at night. Before your head hits the pillow, remember to ask The Universe for a dream, a sign, or a whisper of guidance if you need clarity on a particular subject.

When you learn how to play with the energy of The Universe, you become skilled with your levels of discernment. Once you build trust with this heart-based superpower, you're actively engaging in the magic and beauty of life.

Dear Universe,

I deeply honor my intuitive feelings. I remember to listen to the eternal flow of guidance and support from my higher self in my times of need. I trust in the clarity of my inner vision to discern the appropriate path of inspired action to take.
So be it, so it is.

---

53 JOYFUL

FEELING JOYFUL IS one of the most vibrant and beautiful states of flow and well-being to occupy. When you are fully engaged in the energy of joy, you are being completely present in the moment. The Universe is flowing through you, and the consciousness of humanity is expanding with each tiny moment of appreciation. The buoyancy of joy is a powerful currency in the creation process. It's fun, playful, youthful, and exuberant. You're looking at the bright side of life and seeing the silver linings of the clouds.

Remember

BEING IN A state of joy is your number 1 daily priority in order to live a life of meaning, presence, and purpose.

If you're looking to manifest more joy into your life, look for things to appreciate at least three times a day. Also consider making a playlist of music that you can dance to. Joy is usually activated by moving your body and allowing your head to step aside and your heart to jump into the driver's seat. Remember to surround yourself with things and objects that bring you joy. If something doesn't, donate it to someone who would love it more than you do.

One of the most powerful ways to spark joy is to commit a random act of kindness for a total stranger. There is something super-magical about doing something nice for someone else without expecting anything in return. Try it and see for yourself! Joy is always sparked by kindness.

Dear Universe,

I am so connected to the flow of joy in my life. I am totally open to more fun and excitement manifesting into my reality that I can deeply appreciate and feel grateful for. May my joy and kindness inspire joy and kindness in others.
So be it, so it is.

 LOVED

WHAT MAKES YOU feel loved? When you feel loved, the whole world seems like a much kinder place, a place where you don't feel so alone.

Remember

THE UNIVERSE ADORES who you are now and who you are in the process of becoming. You are so loved and so cherished.

Being able to receive love is vitally important. When you enter into a relationship of any kind, it becomes a system of mutual support. It requires nurturing, balance, and the sensory awareness of when to help solve problems versus when to offer pure, unconditional support.

Feeling loved means that your desired love language has been expressed correctly. For instance, I adore fresh flowers. On the eighth anniversary of when I met my soulmate, Sean, he surprised me with two bunches of roses and a potted orchid. In fact, he buys me a new orchid every few weeks because he knows that makes me feel loved. I also feel loved when he makes a cup of coffee, or when he tells me I look beautiful in the morning when my hair looks like a bird's nest!

One of the most powerful questions you can ask yourself is how you can make someone you care about feel loved. What can you do to support them? How can you initiate connection at a deeper level?

I also like to make sure that my children feel loved on a daily basis, so there is not a day that goes by where I don't hug or kiss them and thank them for being in my life. Being loved and giving love is the way The Universe expresses life through us. This expands the consciousness of the planet and is the metaphysical oxygen that ensures humanity can breathe.

Dear Universe,

I am so loved. Every cell in my entire being sings when I can openly receive a gesture of love. I also completely love and accept myself exactly as I am. I am worthy to give and receive love.
So be it, so it is.

55 LOVING

"Being deeply loved by someone gives you strength, while loving someone deeply gives you courage."
— LAO TZU

WHEN EMBRACING THE energy of being loving, you must tune in to what you want to express as opposed to what you believe the act of loving will create. So many people say "I love you" almost as if it's a question. They say it as a way to gauge feedback that they are indeed in a mutually loving relationship.

Being loving is the energy of service without expecting anything in return. It's perfecting the art of selflessness. It's how The Universe flows through us at all times.

Remember

IF YOU CAN always come from the space of being loving, you are coming from a place of compassion. You are also sparking the magical connection that binds humanity.

People show and express love in so many different ways. The true spiritual work is when you can show up and be loving despite what you are being told or presented with. If you can hold space with non-judgment and compassion, you become the embodiment of loving action in divine service.

Dear Universe,

Show me ways that I can be more loving in my life, whether it's toward myself or my loved ones. Guide me to remember that the power of love and compassion is what holds the fabric of humanity together. Being loving is my natural state.
So be it, so it is.

56 LUCKY

ONE COULD ARGUE that there is no such thing as luck — that we create our own destiny and that we're all living out a sacred contract that we penned with The Universe prior to being born. I believe that destiny is movable by nature. It changes, shifts direction, and restructures itself based on how emotions are guided.

Remember

LUCK IS SIMPLY the energy of activated abundance and the awareness that an event that manifested was auspicious and divinely orchestrated.

One evening, Sean and I were leaving a Chinese restaurant in Las Vegas to get into our car and drive home. All of a sudden we heard aggressive voices from over a construction fence yelling abuse at us. It was a bunch of rowdy teenage boys. I quickly got into the car and Sean went around the other side of the vehicle to get into the driver's seat. Then I heard what sounded like a gunshot.

The kids had hurled a brick over the fence in Sean's direction. It was only an inch away from hitting his skull. The impact would have killed him instantly. Instead, it smashed the taillight of our car. Can you imagine how I felt in that moment? Lucky. I felt so darn lucky that The Universe didn't allow the brick and my husband's skull to cross paths. But is it luck, or it is divine intervention? It's a similar question to whether or not it was the chicken that came first, or the egg.

Luck and divine intervention are the same thing — the essence of grace. It's Lady Luck at her best and the force of The Universe reminding you that anything is possible.

Dear Universe,

I now draw good fortune my way, into every area of my reality. Thank you for allowing me to tune in to the energetic flow of limitless possibilities. I feel so grateful for the blessings and favorable conditions in my life.
So be it, so it is.

---

57 MAGICAL

LIFE IS MAGICAL. You can tune in to this magic and feel the essence of the powerful source of life flowing through you all the time.

Remember

YOU MAKE YOUR own magic. If you ask The Universe to send you magic, then you must believe in magic at all times. Seek first the world of the wondrous and all things shall be added unto you.

Kids have this critical component of life all figured out. Their little eyes light up when they see something they deem magical. The holiday season is the perfect example of how children get swept up in the magic of giving, connection, wonder, awe, and limitless possibilities. So why do we only reserve magic-sparking for a few days of the year? You must see the world of wonder and magic through the eyes of a child.

When I was a child, I loved the idea of magic. My wild imagination would run away with me sometimes because I was so fascinated by all things mystical and magical. I adored the idea of different realms where the fairies lived and that wishes could come true. In fact, I never really stopped believing in that, and I highly encourage you to re-spark magic in your own life. You can do this by allowing fun to flow more freely in your life. Dress up, decorate, buy a wand, celebrate, give presents, create surprises, commit random acts of kindness (lots of them), wear glitter, listen to Tchaikovsky's "Dance of the Sugar Plum Fairy," look at the stars at night and make a wish if you see a shooting star, pick wild flowers, decorate your yard in solar fairy lights (and not just during the holidays) — the creative possibilities are endless! Magic is everywhere and anything you make it!

Dear Universe,

I am fully engaged in the magic of life. Thank you for allowing me the insight and wisdom to have access to the world of wonder. I see my reality through the eyes of a child and spark the magic of possibilities.
So be it, so it is.

58 MOTIVATED

MOTIVATION IS A powerful force. It can help create transformation, inspiration, or impact—in either your own life or the lives of others. When you are motivated, you are usually purpose-driven to manifest meaningful change into your reality.

Remember

TRUE MOTIVATION IS sparked in your life when you are ready to consistently take inspired action. This intention then snowballs and builds the momentum you require to manifest results.

What motivates you the most in life? When you reflect on this question, you can gain a greater sense of clarity about your mission and purpose on the planet. Are you motivated by money? Are you motivated by altruistic pursuits? Are you motivated by pain, because it's too painful for something in your life to stay the same right now? Pain is one of the most powerful intrinsic motivators and catalysts for change.

To be clear—motivation is a close cousin of intention. The two play together very well. In fact, where intention is the vision, motivation is the rocket fuel that drives the desire home. So in order to spark motivation in your life, you need to learn how to gently push yourself to take action. It's super-easy to not go to the gym. It's super-easy to not enroll in that course, make that phone call, clear out the garage, or send that follow-up email. Motivation is a flow of infinite possibilities, and when you ride the wave of this energy, it takes you to exciting new opportunities and places. The first step? Identify what motivates you, and then create a game plan in your journal to list out all of the things that will support you to feel motivated and inspired.

Dear Universe,

I am an open channel for the ongoing momentum of motivation.
Allow me to take inspired action on a regular basis to create the
results that I desire to see manifest into my reality.
So be it, so it is.

59 MOVED

WHEN YOU FEEL moved, it's as if your heartstrings have been pulled and The Universe is sweeping you up into a moment of the appreciation of true beauty. It could be that you are touched by the kind gesture of a stranger. You might have watched a YouTube video of a dying husband's last words to his wife. Perhaps you heard news of a charity that has made a huge impact on the world. Feeling moved is the truest and purest essence of inspiration and transformation.

Remember

THE MORE YOU can feel moved in your life, the more you live life from the energy of your heart space. This allows you to connect with people on a deeper and more meaningful level.

When my daughter Lulu was about five weeks old, I was invited to my mother's concert at a local church hall. My mother had been driving hours upon hours each week to take opera singing lessons, and she was so keen to have me come and experience one of her performances. I had never seen my mother sing before, let alone in front of a crowd of over 60 people!

The conductor introduced her to the audience. She stood there — statu-esque — with a beautiful colorful wrap draped over her shoulder. She was accompanied by a full orchestra. Apparently, the entire song was from a famous Italian opera about a failed romance. As soon as my mother (Louise) began to sing, I could feel tears welling up because I felt so moved emotionally by her beauty and her musical gift. I was moved by her confidence and by her ability to sing so powerfully and to overcome the mental barriers of feeling scared to do something so wildly out of her comfort zone.

Feeling moved by anything is a gift from The Universe to be enjoyed and also documented. Write down the things, people, places, and experiences that move you on a soul level. This is a treasure map for unlocking miracles in every area of your life.

Dear Universe,

Send me experiences that move me on a soul level. May I be surrounded with loved ones to share these moments with, so that magical memories are created and cherished forever.
So be it, so it is.

> "Let food be thy medicine and medicine be thy food."
> — HIPPOCRATES

FEELING NOURISHED ON every level of your being is the fastest avenue to wellness in body, mind, and spirit. Nourishment extends beyond the food we choose to eat to include the stimuli we allow to enter into our conscious minds. This means that if you are constantly reading, engaging in, or watching stories of horror and other violence, then you are not nourishing your mind and protecting your consciousness from upsetting imagery. I always cover my eyes in horror movies and TV shows where there is gratuitous violence. Studies show that this kind of imagery does have an effect on your subconscious mind. It causes the chemical cortisol to flood your bloodstream and block nourishment. Having said that though, it's important to be realistic. Keeping up with the news is an example of the opportunity to guide your perspective and offer compassion.

Remember

WHATEVER YOU CHOOSE to put into your body and allow into your mind will either nourish your soul or weaken your connection to The Universe. It's all about your perspective and the energy you bring to the situation.

I believe there is a strong connection in the relationship we have with food and the relationship we have with The Universe. Food is fuel to keep our bodies healthy and energized, and to remind us to be grateful for the nourishment that appears in our reality on a daily basis. Nourishment is the extension of love that The Universe has for us, which is why it's so important to make it a priority.

As a daily practice, give thanks to the elements that help grow your food — to the sun, the air, the water, the workers, and to the energy of abundance that gives you the choice to support your life through adequate nourishment. Allow this to be your meditation of gratitude:

Dear Universe,

I give thanks for the nourishment that fuels the life force within me.
I honor my awareness to make healthy choices and I am committed to guiding my energy to a state of constant wellness. And if I do sometimes choose pizza or wine, that self-compassion becomes my nourishment and the blessing that I am able to choose again another time.
So be it, so it is.

61 OPEN

THE FEELING OF being open is so much better that being closed-minded. If you truly open your heart and mind to new opportunities and experiences, The Universe is able to deliver you more exciting adventures to cherish. Life becomes more meaningful.

Gary and Gloria had a son named Marcus. Their only child and the light of their lives, Marcus was in his final year of high school, and Gloria was concerned that he wasn't going to attend the prom because he never mentioned any girls that he liked. Gary was a retired football player and owned a pool cleaning company. He would often find himself wondering why Marcus was so introverted and private.

"Have you got a girlfriend yet?" Gary would often inquire.

Marcus played chess and loved hockey, Japanese anime, and collecting comics — but his parents had never met any of his friends.

Then one day Gary asked his son a question he had always been terrified to ask because he was aware of his lack of openness:

"Son, are you gay?"

Marcus froze and replied quietly: "No . . . I'm bisexual. I like girls and guys."

Gary and Gloria both got up out of their chairs and wrapped their arms around their son. As parents, they both acknowledged how much they loved Marcus and that they would support him in any way he needed.

Remember

BEING OPEN MEANS that you can show up with love and compassion in times when your friends and family need support.

Dear Universe,

Open my heart and my mind to see beyond judgment. Allow me to recognize my blind spots and explore the spaces where I could be more inclusive. I am open to new people, new places, and new possibilities.

So be it, so it is.

62 PASSIONATE

WHAT EXCITES YOU? What lights you up on the inside and inspires you to take action? Passion is a palpable force that drives people to create beautiful things and experiences. When you feel passionate, you are incredibly present with the process. You are fully engaged in the essence of joy, of love, and of motivation. Passion is fuel for your emotional state to move forward. It pushes you toward an outcome that you hold very dearly to your heart. Whether it's spiritual activism, art, lovemaking, poetry, or getting your ideas heard by one person or the entire world, the concept of passion is the truest encapsulation of divine energy in action.

Remember

ONLY YOU CAN define what you are passionate about. It's a beautiful gift to choose to channel your energy into the direction you know will create powerful change.

I adore the energy and passion of people who are committed to manifesting change for people who are suffering. When passion and service unite, it brings out the best in humanity. It shows us that we can do anything we put our hearts and minds to when we come together. Passion always fans the flames to create radical and meaningful change. So if you're wanting to spark and ignite more passion in your life, pause to ask yourself how you can help and what you're willing to support. What are your values? How can you be of service to others to join the energy of passion? What is your life's passion project? How can The Universe support you?

Dear Universe,

May the energy of passion manifest into my reality so that I feel inspired to create something magical in my life and the lives of others. May I feel the energy of passion fuel my motivation and open my heart to all possibilities.
So be it, so it is.

225

63 PEACEFUL

YOU MUST ALLOW space in your life to be peaceful. The feeling is incredibly important to live a life of wellness, love, and joy. If you can stay calm, cool, and collected in the eye of a storm, and remain peaceful within your heart, then you have mastered one of the most valuable lessons of being here on earth.

Remember

FEELING PEACEFUL IS a powerful state to be in.

It's so important to reduce stress and seek relaxation as much as you can in your daily life. Stress is a silent health risk for most people. However, if you switch your attention to the power of manifesting peace, you will experience more happiness and wellness. The good news is that you get to choose what you find peaceful and relaxing. It could be taking a walk in the park, doing a meditation, watching a TV show, or cooking a beautiful meal. Inner peace can be found as soon as you pause and remind yourself of your power to guide your energy and your emotions.

Every moment that you connect to the presence of The Universe will bring you peace.

Dear Universe,

May peace always prevail and reveal itself to be the path of least resistance. May my actions, deeds, and words always come from a space of compassion for the sake of peace.
So be it, so it is.

 PLAYFUL

THE UNIVERSE LOVES it when you are playful because play instantly manifests a sense of happiness and joy and creates space in your life to welcome in more fun. The more playful you can be in your life, the more you are actually living a joyous life.

You get 100 years to live (if you're lucky), and yet adults get so easily weighed down by the more serious aspects of life — work, bills, politics, the future . . . and the list goes on!

Remember

IF YOU CAN get out of your head and into your heart, you'll be in a prime state to engage in the art of playfulness.

It works wonders in relationships. Also, most children would love for their parents to be more playful and fun. The key is to do things outside of your comfort zone. In summer, have water fights. Play more games. Allow yourself to laugh and see the humorous side of life. Your experience has been designed by The Universe to be a divine comedy.

For instance, my husband, Sean, and I were feeling a bit sad and depressed late one evening because we didn't have enough money to pay our bills. It was winter 2012. I had the crazy idea that we go outside into our private courtyard, get naked, and throw pots of cold water on one another to see if it would make us laugh. Sure enough it did! We were laughing hysterically because the experience was so hilarious, ridiculous, and exhilarating! So no matter how ridiculous your idea may sound, try it! You must interrupt the mental patterns, the limiting beliefs, and the programming that says that you can't be playful or that you're too old. Life is way too short to not laugh at least once a day.

Dear Universe,

Show me creative ideas and ways that I can have more fun with my friends and my loved ones. Allow my whole heart to laugh and enjoy joyful experiences as a way to keep my spirits high.
So be it, so it is.

 POSITIVE

FEELING POSITIVE IS an excellent space to occupy within your heart. If you can remember to always look on the bright side of life, it's impossible for party poopers to bring you down.

Remember

THE POWER OF positivity can transform your reality very quickly.

Quite often, events and situations will happen in your life that you label "negative." Just remember that most clouds have a silver lining if you look long enough. There are also many blessings in disguise if you are willing to see your current situation as temporary.

It's also important to be mindful that you can't (and shouldn't) be 100 percent super positive all the time. It's virtually impossible to be all rainbows, glitter, and unicorns during every event of your life. You need to and must experience contrasting energy in order to move you forward. Manifestation cannot happen without the highs and the lows — you need the ups and the downs in order to propel you forward into a vibrant and exciting new reality. Always ask The Universe to guide you back to the awareness that there is a silver lining for your cloud . . .

Dear Universe,

I trust that whatever I am experiencing right now will have a positive outcome. I now remember that I get to choose and guide my energy. May I set the intention to look for positive things to feel grateful for.
So be it, so it is.

66 POWERFUL

YOU ARE A powerful human being. If you live a life devoted to joy, take inspired action from your heart, be of service to humanity, and hold compassion for others, then you are incredibly powerful. Too often people push their power to the side and brush it off as if it's a piece of fluff or lint on their shoulder. We're told that power is bad and that we are separate from The Universe.

Remember

WHEN YOU EMBRACE your power, you can begin to consciously create your own reality. The landscape of your life will literally bend and transfigure around you.

The pure essence of feeling powerful can radically transform your state of mind. You no longer operate from a paradigm of fear, and you can deliberately guide your energy to manage your emotions more wisely. True power is in remembering that you are in the driver's seat of your soul and The Universe is your copilot.

Many people believe that external forces are responsible for what shows up in their lives. They forget that they are a magnificent continuum of the power of The Universe. Since everything is energy, the beliefs you hold around owning your own power will determine whether life happens to you, rather than through you.

Affirm to yourself on a daily basis that you are powerful. It's your divine birthright to claim your power and use it to consciously construct your own reality.

Dear Universe,

I am a powerful being. I own the power I have to create my own reality. I embrace the power within my heart to lead with love at all times. I tune in to the essence of my power to ask for guidance, wisdom, and inspired ideas. My power source is supercharged when I connect with the energetic flow of limitless possibilities. My power is magnified when I am being of service to others.
So be it, so it is.

67 PRESENT

IF YOU ARE feeling present right now in this moment, you are at the most powerful and pivotal point of creation. The gift of feeling present is where the magic of The Universe is revealed to you.

Remember

WHEN YOU CATCH yourself being aware of the present moment and the power of now, you catch a glimpse of who you truly are. You remember your superpowers.

Many people tend to live in the past — it's already happened, and yet they keep rehashing it over and over again and wishing things could have been different. Many people tend to hang out in the daydream space of the future, too, because they are hoping that things will transform and be radically different than they are now. The key piece to hold in your heart is that if you can be present with whatever shows up in your current reality, and you feel grateful for it, then The Universe can flow through you with more miracles.

Think of moments in your life that you have been the most present. Write down in your journal the Top Ten Present Moments of your life thus far. Some of mine include holding my children for the first time as they glanced up at me — their tiny fingers curled around my little finger. I was 100 percent present when I married my soulmate and recited my vows from my heart to his. I'm present during meditation, when I enjoy a beautiful glass of red wine or a delicious meal, view an exquisite piece of artwork, or am in a flow state when I'm writing. Any time you are present, you are standing in the beauty of the moment in unified agreeance with The Universe. This is the essence of love.

Dear Universe,

I am now aware of the stillness and the presence within this moment. Allow my entire being to relax into this energy of surrender. May it carry restorative properties and may it heal the temptation not to be present. I now go with the flow and witness how being present can soothe my soul on so many levels.
So be it, so it is.

68 PROSPEROUS

IF YOU ARE in a state of feeling prosperous, you are magnetizing your current situation and attracting more prosperity into your reality.

Remember

THE MORE YOU can tune in and allow yourself to feel the full flow of abundance in life, the more prosperity will be drawn to you.

The feeling of being prosperous can be very subjective. For instance, when I was a single mother living below the poverty line, I felt so grateful and prosperous when my welfare checks landed in my bank account. It symbolized that I had made it through another two weeks. True wealth is about encapsulating the essence of gratitude for whatever shows up in your life.

Back in 2010, Sean and I were mentored by a guy who apparently had over a billion dollars in contracts pass over his desk. It was an urban myth around the local community that he was down to his last $100 million and was struggling to make ends meet. For a "normal" human, his fear might seem totally ridiculous. You see, it's all about perspective and either adopting the mind-set of abundance or the mind-set that is based on scarcity.

Some of us also hold the energy of guilt around wanting to feel prosperous. We keep the energy of the possibility well away from the likelihood of actually manifesting into our lives in order to make ourselves (and others) feel comfortable. I remind my Manifesting Academy students all the time that money is energy. It's a transaction of currency in exchange for consciousness (which is energy). The more you can feel prosperous and believe that you are attracting abundance into your life, the more freedom you will ultimately experience.

Dear Universe,

I declare to the energy of all that is, that I am prosperous. My mind-set is focused on abundance and I believe there is enough prosperity for everyone. I give myself full permission to live a life of financial freedom in a way that nurtures my soul with meaning and contribution. Reveal to me a path of inspired ideas to explore. **So be it, so it is.**

100 MINI-MEDITATIONS TO EMBRACE LOVE

WHEN YOU FEEL protected, it helps you relax and trust that you will not come into harm's way at all. I believe that most of us, if not all of us, are divinely protected by our spirit guides or our angels. I have read way too many stories of people narrowly escaping potentially fatal experiences to not trust that we have special "helpers" from the nonphysical realm guiding us to a path of safety.

Remember

CARRY THE BELIEF in your heart that you are guided and protected at all times. The more you trust in this belief, the safer you will feel.

In Australia one day, Sean and I were running a little late to pick up the kids from school. He was driving, and there was nowhere to park. I told him to stop, and I would just jump out so he could circle back and pick me up when I had the kids. Just as I was about to open the door, I heard a voice in my head say: "NO!"

My body froze, and I paused. In that moment of pausing, a bus was speeding past in the wrong lane. Had I opened the door and stepped out into the street I would have been killed instantly.

It's these beautiful soulful whispers and intuitive nudges in our times of need that save our butts from being placed in grave danger. I felt so grateful that I was protected in that moment — someone was looking out for me! In your daily gratitude list always remember to include a little love note to the beings that offer protection.

Dear Universe,

Thank you for working with my guides and angels to keep me protected and safe. I trust that all is unfolding as it should and that I am kept out of harm's way — sheltered and protected from the storms of life at this point in time.

So be it, so it is.

---

(70) PROUD

SOME OF US have been taught that being prideful is a bad thing. I believe there is nothing wrong with giving yourself a pat on the back and feeling proud of your achievements or accomplishments. When you can get to a space where you feel proud for the journey you have traveled, you know that you are living life to the fullest.

I am such a proud parent. In 2018, my son, Thomas, invited me to come and watch him compete in a Japanese speaking contest at a local high school. They announced his name, and he confidently walked onto the stage holding the microphone to give a five-minute speech, completely in fluent Japanese. I had no idea what he was saying, but the crowd laughed at least three times! In that moment I was so very proud of him — of everything he had been through in his life up to that point.

Remember

PRIDE WELLS UP within your heart because it's the acknowledgment that the present moment you are experiencing represents truth, and that a powerful chapter has unfolded.

We're all on a journey to authentically express who we truly are in the world. We need the space to do this without fear of judgment. Feeling proud of the journey we have experienced and who we have become on the journey is so vital for The Universe to express divine energy through us.

Dear Universe,

I am so proud of this moment. I am so proud of who I am and who I am in the process of becoming. May I celebrate the successes of others in my life, and also celebrate my own achievements from a space of humility, thankfulness, and gratitude.
So be it, so it is.

(71) RELAXED

SOMETIMES THE MOST productive thing you can do is relax.

Remember

THE TRUE ESSENCE of relaxation is activated by leaning into the beautiful wholeness of life and taking care of yourself first.

Most people keep themselves on edge way too much. They drink too much coffee, don't get enough sleep, or allow stress to overshadow their happiness. You must make time to unwind in your life and relax about the things you are wanting to manifest.

To do this you must spark a self-care routine that allows you to nurture yourself and to unwind from the demands of daily life.

Ideas to begin this process include getting a massage, cooking a nutritious meal, or taking a warm bath. Or try going out into nature. The stillness and the lack of sound and distractions is what will help you to recalibrate your soul the most quickly. I live right near a place called Red Rock Canyon in Las Vegas. On Sean's birthday in 2017, we went for a hike in the desert. We walked for about an hour into the mountains — stepping over stones, rocks, and the occasional cactus blooming in bright-pink petals. The peacefulness was so calming, and we felt so relaxed. There was no noise and no electronic interference — just bliss and space to relax.

What will make you feel the most relaxed? Take out some paper and a pen and write a list of things you can do within the next 12 hours that will help you to unwind from the demands of daily life.

Dear Universe,

Show me ways that I can relax and enjoy the present moment.
Allow my entire being to surrender and to feel a sense of relaxation in order to spark a renewed sense of energy in my life. May I remember that relaxation is a vital part of my daily self-care routine.
So be it, so it is.

 **RELIEVED**

NOTHING IS SWEETER than the feeling of relief—especially when you are uncomfortable, itchy, bursting to use the bathroom, or uncertain as to how a situation is going to play itself out. Feeling relieved is usually paired with the thought that perhaps you weren't in such a terrible or difficult situation after all.

Remember

IF YOU FEEL relieved, thank The Universe for supporting you on your journey with a favorable outcome. Gratitude for "what is" will transform your experience of relief into a meaningful memory.

In 2014, I had lost a total of five pregnancies in eight months, and I was just a little over five weeks pregnant, again. One afternoon I began to show and feel all of the signs that the pregnancy was headed in the direction of another loss. Sean drove me to the emergency room. The time it takes at the hospital to see a doctor can sometimes be hours of arduous waiting and waiting. The time drags—and the dog-eared magazines in the waiting room are filled with happy celebrity baby stories, which are like rubbing salt on a wound.

After a few hours Sean had to leave to pick up our kids from school. I was feeling okay, and told him that I knew what to expect and would be fine.

Another hour passed, and I decided to take out my phone and write a message to the baby. This was an attempt at calming myself and getting my heart into a good space of being open to all possibilities. I wrote:

It's going to be okay. I love you. Be safe. I'm grateful for you. I'm grateful to The Universe no matter what happens. It is my honor to carry you. No matter what the outcome, I am here, I am well, you are safe.

Then the doctor called my name to scan my belly. On the screen showed a beautiful little bean with a healthy strong heartbeat at just five weeks and three days old. The relief of seeing the life force in action was so sweet. I fell deeply in love with that tiny heart, and on the day Lulu Dawn was born, I finally felt another level and layer of relief once she was finally safe at home in my arms.

Ask The Universe to provide relief in your times of need. The fastest way to remedy your feelings of fear and anxiety is to accept that you will be okay, no matter what the outcome. All will be well.

Dear Universe,

Thank you for this experience. May I lean into the energy of relief by remembering that I have a choice on how I wish to guide my energy. I choose to embrace love and rise above fear. This brings me a sense of calm and a sense of relief.
So be it, so it is.

73 RESTED

WHEN YOU FEEL adequately rested, you feel like you're at your best. You're ready to deal with any situation The Universe sends in your direction. Rest and relaxation are super-important elements of your daily self-care routine and rituals.

The main element to consider is what activities or support you require in order to give your body the things it needs to feel more rejuvenated. Your well-being in body, mind, and spirit will thrive when given the time needed to sink into the present moment and release the tension that creates unnecessary hurdles in our lives.

Remember

FEELING RESTED MAKES you feel energized and uplifted and gives you the foundation you require to create a magnificent life of intention.

Lack of rest can hinder us in all sorts of ways. Our health and wellness can suffer. Our emotions might feel out of balance, and our bodies will give us very clear messages when we're not slowing down as much as we need to.

Take time in your day for a nap or some quiet time away from electronics or distractions. Other ideas include taking a hot bath, going to bed an hour early for a week, not drinking so much coffee, or treating yourself to a massage. These are all creative ways to support you on your quest for more rest.

The Universe wants you to chill out and go with the flow. Meditation is also a great way to get some much needed rest and relaxation . . .

Dear Universe,

Throughout the day I feel vibrant and energized. I am aware that resting and relaxing are the keys to feeling grounded in the present moment. I now make healthy choices for my body that are based on taking care of myself. I am rested and rejuvenated.
So be it, so it is.

74 REVERENT

IF YOU ARE currently experiencing feeling reverent, or if you are seeking ways to spark the essence of reverence, the core foundation is activated by being respectful. Reverence is the deep and powerful understanding of appreciation for the cosmic forces that create your reality. Whether you call this power The Universe, God, Source, The Almighty — the respect you feel in your heart will strengthen your connection.

Remember

WHEN YOU ACKNOWLEDGE The Universe as your cofounder, your cocreator, and your copilot, it sends more creative and collaborative magic for you to experience and play with in your life.

Reverence is most easily shown during meditation or prayer. By thanking The Universe for everything that is delivered into your reality, you open your heart to new and exciting possibilities. It also helps to remind you that you're not in this life adventure alone — The Universe is helping you, guiding you, and offering you a steady stream of wisdom on your path.

Use this meditation as a way to engage in the beauty of reverence:

> ### Dear Universe,
>
> Thank you for everything that has happened in my life. I know and trust that you are guiding and protecting me on my journey. I deeply appreciate and feel profoundly grateful for the wisdom and intuitive whispers you have sent in my direction.
> **So be it, so it is.**

75 SAFE

HUMANS USUALLY HOLD in their hearts a desire to manifest three things: safety, control, and approval. It's your basic human right to feel safe in your life, but sometimes it's not guaranteed. You might not feel as if you have a safe space to express your thoughts or emotions in a relationship. You might not feel safe walking back to your car from yoga at 10 p.m. You might not feel safe with the choices you make and the boundaries you set with yourself.

Remember

MORE OFTEN THAN not, there are beautiful lessons of wisdom that are unveiled when we seek safety. When we do feel safe, we have the awareness that life can shift very fast and that we must be prepared to go with the flow and naturally adapt to the present moment.

There have been many times in my life where I have felt unsafe. Throughout my volatile relationship with my ex-husband Max, I decided to continue to live with him in a bizarre attempt to heal the relationship. During that time, I felt so unsafe. However, many months later, when I did finally make the decision to leave, I felt so safe and sound. For the first time in many years, I could sleep peacefully without the threat of violence or emotional pain. When you feel safe, you feel free.

Always, and I mean always, turn to The Universe when you hold the desire to feel safe. Also, please seek assistance if your physical safety is at risk in any way. There is no shame in reaching out for help.

Dear Universe,

I desire to feel safe. Reveal to me the empowered path to seek safety in my current situation. May I trust that the right people and resources will manifest to support and assist me on my journey.
So be it, so it is.

---

76 SATISFIED

WHEN YOU FEEL satisfied, it's as if everything is well in your world. Nothing more is needed or required to declare an experience as a "perfect moment." Satisfaction can be experienced in so many wonderful ways — when you get a triple-word score in Scrabble, when you collect all of the coins in Super Mario, when you finally get that tiny piece of seaweed out of your back tooth, or when you experience a full-circle moment — satisfaction is oh-so-sweet. It reminds you that nothing in life ever stays the same and that life is seasonal, and so you need to celebrate the times when you can snapshot a moment of perfection in your mind.

Remember

SATISFACTION IS BECAUSE all of the boxes on your list of requirements have been ticked. You've hit your milestones and scored your goals, your rules have been adhered to, and there is beautiful alignment and harmony in place.

Many people leave reviews on blogs, shopping websites, and other customer service avenues that allow space to display dissatisfaction with a product or service. How often do you take time to leave reviews that you are satisfied with your experience? Have you ever seen this as a gesture of gratitude and had that energy echoed back to you? Make it your mission within the next 24 hours to express that you are satisfied, and watch what manifests next.

Dear Universe,

Show me moments where I can identify that I am satisfied
and everything feels in alignment. Remind me that gratitude is a close
relative of satisfaction, so the more I can feel content, the more you
will deliver experiences to appreciate into my reality.
So be it, so it is.

77 SEEN

MY HUSBAND, SEAN, and I tried a little experiment that had some surprising results. For the last month of my pregnancy with Lulu in 2015, we took a vow of silence in our bedroom. That meant that there was to be no verbal communication between us at all. Our goal was to generate the energy of sacred space in our bedroom and to truly "see" one another.

The reason we tried this was because too often couples suffer because they don't create space for quality, meaningful, connected time with one another. We're always on our phones or watching TV. There sometimes isn't enough eye contact and full attentiveness. This experiment transformed our bedroom into a place of rest, rejuvenation, and meaningful connection.

Remember

BEING SEEN IS a two-way street. You must allow yourself to be visible in order to be seen at a soul level.

When someone truly sees who you are inside your heart and in the core of your soul, you become connected. This is the name of the game when it comes to life. You can either move toward unity (love) or separation (fear).

Allowing yourself to feel seen is the first step in having more meaningful connections with other beautiful humans out there in the world.

Dear Universe,

I feel seen by my loved ones. I feel seen by the people I work with in the world. I feel seen by my friends. When I want to spark connection to the soul of the matter with another, I now say these words into their eyes: "I see you." This activates authenticity in the moment to remind us of who we really are.

So be it, so it is.

78 SELFLESS

THERE IS SUCH tremendous beauty in being of service to others without expecting anything in return. Being selfless isn't easy, and it is definitely not for the fainthearted. When you're 100 percent devoted and dedicated to taking care of another human being, that is an act of being selfless.

Parents of a newborn baby or even a brand-new puppy will understand the true nature of selflessness when sleep is interrupted several times per night for a midnight feeding or potty break. Your life is no longer your own, and you wouldn't have it any other way because of the pure unconditional love you experience.

Remember

THE ENERGY YOU bring to an act of service is imperative.

If you desire to be more selfless, look for ways you can contribute time to your family or your local community.

My friend Dallyce told me once that it's her secret project to collect trash on a beach if she sees it. This creative selflessness is really inspiring. Caregivers, nurses, parents, and good-hearted people are contributing to the beautiful energy of the planet by not thinking only of themselves. I remember when Sean ran into the house a few years ago and grabbed a few pairs of his thickest socks for a homeless man he had seen on a corner. The thought of living on the streets of Vegas in winter with cold feet moved Sean to help. You see, compassion is the lifeblood of humanity. When we remember that we're all in this together, it doesn't take a second thought to do something selfless for another human being.

Dear Universe,

Assist me to embody the true essence of being selfless. If I do
something kind, may it not be done to brag about it to anyone (on Instagram)
but rather to quietly know that I am doing my part to contribute
to the fabric of kindness within humanity.
So be it, so it is.

⑲ SENSUAL

FEELING SENSUAL IS such an important element to embrace in order to either nurture your feminine energy or your masculine energy. My dear friend and relationship expert Marla Mattenson introduced me to something she refers to as "the gender spectrum." I love this approach because it means that the energy can ebb and flow and does not need to be fixed based on your gender. Since both sexes embody different energy at different times, this a valuable perspective to consider.

Remember

SENSUALITY IS A deep force of natural wisdom and the embodiment of divine energy and essence.

Sadly, many people have repressed their levels of sensuality due to imbalance, pain, anxiety, or trauma from the past.

In order to begin the healing process and to open your heart to the instant manifestation of sensuality, imagine for a moment that you are sitting on a giant flower. You can see yourself from the outside and you notice that your body is surrounded in a beautiful, glowing purple light. In your mind's eye you now set the intention to free up any energy surrounding the theme of sensuality. Imagine ways that you can be more affectionate and loving through touch, care, experiences, and the appreciation of beauty. How does it feel? How does this impact the intimacy you share in a relationship? How does this impact the relationship you have with yourself?

When you're ready, set this intention with The Universe:

Dear Universe,

I am a sensual being who thrives on touch, intimacy, closeness, and connection. I fully accept all of myself — free from judgment and criticism. I now experience the love that I know and trust that I wholeheartedly deserve.
So be it, so it is.

SERENE

FEELING SERENE IS the calm experienced after the storm. It's that magical experience of tranquility that feels like your entire being is catching a well-deserved break for the first time in a long time.

Remember

THE FEELING OF serenity is so good for your sense of well-being. The more you can tune in and feel serene, the more you can create harmony within your body, your mind, and your spirit.

In 2014, I had lost five pregnancies in a row. We lived in Melbourne, Australia, and I knew that I needed to seek serenity, or I would have a mental breakdown that I felt I could potentially never recover from. My husband, Sean, my two oldest children, and I decided to move back to Noosa, on the coast of Australia. This is where I was living when I fell in love with Sean just a few years earlier. I had moved there to recalibrate my soul after finally leaving Max, so I was aware of the magical healing powers of living by the ocean.

The house we rented was perched on a cliff top overlooking the ocean. The top level was my bedroom, and if you opened all the windows, you could hear the roaring of the ocean waves at night. It was bliss — so serene. We would often see whales, dolphins, and magnificent rainbows. My soul was healing quickly from the soothing connection to the water. Within two weeks of moving to this new house I got pregnant with my daughter Lulu. All it took was seeking serenity and knowing where to find it.

Dear Universe,

Reveal to me the perfect place to seek serenity without,
so I may experience it within. I am fully allowing the energy of peacefulness
and stillness to manifest into my reality.
So be it, so it is.

 SEXY

FEELING SEXY IS incredibly important and not something you should sweep to the side and reject. Sex and lovemaking is how we connect to the important people in our lives. Feeling sexy is the encapsulation of the energy of fun, creativity, the possibility of connection, and also the divine essence of true union. It's when sparks fly and magic happens!

Everyone wants to feel as if they have some level of sex appeal. However, the media bombards us with heavily Photoshopped images of what is commercially deemed to be labeled as "sexy." It's an illusion (mostly based on objectification and stereotyping) designed to generate perfume sales, underwear sales, car sales, and any other product you'd care to imagine. You must not buy into the idea of what external sources categorize as "sexy." Just like you must never fall prey to getting a "beach body" or "bikini body"—because if you're on a beach, then you have a friggin' "beach body." It's a false perspective designed to make you not feel good enough and ultimately cough up your cash.

Remember

YOU GET TO define what you find sexy and how you show up as a person who feels sexy and expresses yourself.

Sexiness is a state of mind.

Sometimes we're so much in our heads about what we think is sexy and what is not that it actually prevents us from being a true expression of what we're really feeling and who we truly are.

Dear Universe,

I fully accept myself for who I am and know that I am super-sexy in my own beautiful way. Guide me to remember that confidence is the key to rising above the illusion that I am not good enough. May I embody the essence of sexiness in my own unique way. I am worthy.

So be it, so it is.

---

82 SOOTHED

WHAT MAKES YOU feel soothed? The feeling of being soothed is really important. As infants, we are supported and nurtured by our parents or care-takers—a pat on the back, cuddles, kisses, unconditional support. As we grow, we are guided to learn how to self-settle.

Remember

LIFE IS FULL of ups and downs. You have a choice of how to soothe your soul without turning to patterns of self-sabotage.

When I was born, my dad made me a blanket which I later dubbed "Cuddly." Cuddly went everywhere with me. By the time I was 18, my security blanket had been loved so much that the knitted pattern and the stitches were unrecognizable. What was once the blanket I was wrapped in when I was first born was now a frayed, gray clump of wool.

In the early days of being married to Max, I would keep a tiny square of Cuddly in my pillowcase. To stop me from crying myself to sleep at night, I sometimes would hold it up against my cheek because it soothed me. Now I find my comfort elsewhere—from dabbing jasmine essential oil on my wrist, to cuddling my children, to pouring a nice glass of red wine to relax after a long day. Figuring out what soothes you means that when life gets frantic (and it will), you have a list of resources in your self-care toolkit to turn to.

Some ideas for feeling soothed include taking a warm bath with Epsom salts, sitting in the sunshine, taking a nap, watching a funny movie, getting a massage, calling a friend—whatever it takes to manifest comfort from the space of taking care of yourself. Of course, meditation is always an excellent way to be soothed by the magic of The Universe . . .

Dear Universe,

Allow me to feel soothed right now so that my concerns, worries, or ailments are washed away. Replace them with the unshakable faith that "this too shall pass" and that balance and well-being are my daily reality.

So be it, so it is.

---

83 STILL

THE TRUE FEELING of stillness is exquisite. Everything in your world feels calm and peaceful, and you trust that The Universe is supporting your intentions in every way. If you can cast your mind back to a time in your life when you felt extreme stillness, then you have a happy place to retreat to in the times of your life that require a moment of peace.

Remember

STILLNESS IS THE pure presence and connection with The Universe. The more you can weave stillness into your life as a daily ritual, the more harmony you will experience.

For me, I imagine the ten-acre property at Red Hill where I spent most of my childhood, from the age of 8 to 18. My parents had a gallery and studio on the mini-farm that overlooked fruit trees, roses, sugar-snap peas, and paddocks of fresh green grass. I would often sit in an apple tree and read a book. When I'd get hungry, I'd just reach for a fresh crunchy apple, pick it, and eat it. Just as the sun was about to go down in the evenings I would stare out at the cherry tree orchard and appreciate the stillness. I would watch the pink petals of the cherry blossoms get carried away on the breeze. I would wonder what adventures I would go on in my life, who I would spend my life with, if I would have children, and who I would become. I knew in those moments that I would one day remember the stillness, the quiet thoughts of inquiry, and be amazed at how much my life had changed since that moment of stillness.

Get curious about your own inner space of stillness. It's from this awareness that you can have a very authentic and real conversation with The Universe.

Dear Universe,

I embody the essence of stillness in my daily life. I am aware that the more time I take to cultivate the feeling of stillness, and to slow down to connect to the present moment, the more I am sparking the magic of possibility.
So be it, so it is.

84 STRONG

YOU ARE SO much stronger than you think you are. When you feel strong, you feel so capable of taking on board any trial or tribulation The Universe sends in your direction.

Remember

BEING STRONG DOESN'T mean that you can't show emotion or express how you're feeling. There is great strength in the vulnerability of shedding tears and asking others for help.

One example is how the hashtag #VegasStrong became the focus of the city following the horrendous massacre that took place in 2017. The community banded together to show strength.

Inner strength is just as powerful and important as physical strength. There have been many documented cases of women who lift impossibly heavy objects to release their children from danger — crazy stories like moving trucks or cars with their bare hands! It's like this inner and innate wisdom takes over their body and they summon as much strength as is humanly possible to deal with the situation.

The interesting and unexpected turns that life takes us on will always require strength. When you find yourself grieving the loss of a loved one, when you find yourself scrambling for pennies to feed yourself for the day, when you feel so depressed you can't lift your head off your pillow — these are all beautiful moments in life that require you to look within and call forth the energy of The Universe to help you manifest a sense of strength to move through your current situation with ease and grace.

Dear Universe,

Give me strength in this moment. I now call forth all of the energy that I have access to in order to step into this situation with grace and confidence. May I now exude the necessary strength to rise above my challenges and be okay. Thank you for giving me all of the strength and resources that I need.

So be it, so it is.

---

85 SUPPORTED

WHEN YOUR GOALS, dreams, wishes, and desires are supported by your loved ones, it helps guide your energy to stay on an inspired path.

Remember

THE UNIVERSE IS always there to support you on your journey.

The Universe will always support you if you take consistent and inspired action. It's as if you have this incredible safety net that is always there for you, without judgment, in your times of need. How you allow The Universe to support you is reflected in direct proportion to how you allow others in your life to support you. If you can receive support, you can dive into the flow of infinite possibilities.

When Louise wanted to divorce Tony, the filing fee for the application was $750 — money that she didn't have. Louise had set the powerful intention and wanted to make the separation of their union official, but had no way of scrambling the money together to make it happen as quickly as she wanted it to. In her mind's eye she was very clear with The Universe that she had set the powerful intention to manifest the money within a week.

In her heart she would chant: "To the wind I say, bring money my way. To the wind I say, bring money my way."

Within just seven days she was offered a job to illustrate a children's book project for the exact amount of $750. You see, when you are clear with your intentions, and you are open for The Universe to support you, it will manifest with ease if you have released the resistance.

Dear Universe,

I remember that I am 100 percent supported on my journey to manifesting. Allow me to receive support, guidance, wisdom, and signs on my path that help keep me grounded on this adventure. May I also support my loved ones and my friends in any way that I am able to do so. I remember that the energy of support and service tunes me in to the flow of infinite wisdom.
So be it, so it is.

86 SURRENDERED

ONE OF THE most vital ingredients in the process of manifestation is to surrender to the powers that be. You must let go of your attachment to things working out exactly as you want them to and hand your trust over to The Universe.

Remember

SURRENDER MEANS THAT you step back from holding on to the illusion that you have control over anything.

You want to manifest money? Surrender to the fact that you may never manifest money. Want to manifest your soulmate? Surrender to the fact you would be perfectly okay living alone. Want to manifest a baby? Be content not being a parent in this lifetime in the traditional way you anticipated. You see, the beauty of playing with the energy of The Universe is to gamify the process and to release the resistance around the intentions. It doesn't mean that these things won't manifest for you, but when you surrender to what is, then magic can happen, and it usually does.

A friend of mine once said, "Infinite patience produces immediate results." The exquisite truth behind this statement is awe-inspiring.

The most powerful way to amplify the energy of surrender is through meditation. In fact, meditation is the act of surrendering and connecting to the divine possibilities within.

Dear Universe,

I now surrender to this moment. I release attachments to outcomes and remember that I cannot control my destiny, I can only guide my energy. I choose to surrender, to relinquish control, and to trust that the divine wisdom of all-that-is is manifesting for the greatest good.
So be it, so it is.

⟨87⟩ THOUGHTFUL

WHEN YOU WANT to manifest the energy of being thoughtful, it's important to be creative with your thinking. Another element to consider is whether or not you are making any assumptions and whether your thoughtfulness will be well received. I once had a guy tell me that he was going to open the door for me at the post office, but he didn't know if I was "a feminist" or not, and if I would get offended by the gesture. See the danger of making assumptions? I told him that I like to open the door for anyone, regardless of gender, because it's an act of kindness.

Remember

BEING THOUGHTFUL IS making life a little easier for someone. You are being of service so the work of The Universe can flow through you.

It's often said that God is in the details. There is no better place to demonstrate this than through acts of thoughtfulness, no matter how big or how small. Simply being more thoughtful and kind in your relationship will help to strengthen your union. Gestures of thoughtfulness could be as simple as bringing your loved one a glass of water before bed, holding the door for a stranger, or cooking a meal for a family with a newborn baby. It feels so good to be fully engaged in the art of thoughtfulness — it can spark some serious magic.

Dear Universe,

Guide me to an inspired path that allows me to express more
thoughtfulness in my life. How can I show up in creative ways of kindness
that will help to support my friends, loved ones, and strangers?
Guide me and I will graciously follow.
So be it, so it is.

---

88 TOLERANT

I SEE OTHERS wishing to manifest a sense of tolerance for people and events in their lives all the time. Tolerating can sometimes be settling for a situation that is less than desirable, but I selected this emotion to be placed in the "Embrace Love" section because there are many people out there who aspire to be more tolerant.

Don't get me wrong, we could all learn how to be more tolerant on the subjects of different beliefs and perspectives. However, there are people who are tolerant to their own detriment — especially in personal relationships.

Remember

WHAT YOU MANIFEST is what you tolerate.

If you're willing to accept feelings, habits, or beliefs that are different from your own, then that's very noble, but not if it's at the expense of your own sense of self.

The epitome of someone who is tolerant and embodies the essence of tolerance is perhaps someone who works in the complaints department at a company. All day long, they have to deal with angry and disgruntled customers who are expressing irritation.

You do not have to manifest the energy of being tolerant. Patient, yes — because patience, as we all know, is a very virtuous trait. Being tolerant is your opportunity to see if you are truly embodying the principles of acceptance or throwing your sense of self under the bus.

Dear Universe

Allow me to examine the elements that I tolerate in my life that could be profoundly transformed by a subtle shift in my energy. Show me ways that I can exhibit kindness and compassion without losing my sense of self.
So be it, so it is.

89 TRANSFORMATIVE

WHEN YOU CAN see yourself in an intentional transformative phase, life becomes more magical and exciting. You might be trying to educate yourself to learn something new. You might be trying to build strength in your body through exercise. Or perhaps you are learning new techniques to bring to a relationship for more peace and harmony in your daily life. The key is to be committed to being a lifelong learner — always changing and committed to personal growth.

Kaizen (改善) is the Japanese word for "improvement" or "change for the better." This philosophy has been incorporated into various life-coaching and psychotherapy models as a state to aspire to. When we are committed to conscious transformation in our lives, it brings us powerful meaning and connection to the world around us.

From the moment you entered the world as a tiny baby, you have been embarking on the most wonderful adventure of consistent change. Due to the nature of all life being cyclic, it's a powerful reminder that transformation is inevitable. In fact, you're not the same person you were five minutes ago, let alone five years ago. New cells are being created, new thoughts are being formed, and the reality around you and within you is perpetually manifesting newness.

Remember

TO CELEBRATE AND welcome transformation into your life, you must honor your growth and development. Upon reflection, you will see that life is an ever-evolving journey of creation.

Dear Universe,

May I remember that the seasons of my life are a natural and imperative element of my soul's journey. May I welcome new change into my life and honor the cyclic nature of the human experience.
So be it, so it is.

TRUSTING

TRUST IS A beautiful feeling. When you wholeheartedly trust a person or a situation or The Universe, life flows more effortlessly for you. When you lack trust or you base your current situation on the echoes of the past, that creates pain.

Remember

IF YOU CAN'T trust people, you can't trust The Universe. This is like turning your back on investing in your wellness. Trusting at a deep level that everything is working out for the greatest good will help to spark inspiration into every area of your life.

Take Elvie, for example. She lived in a small apartment in New Zealand with her cat, Roy. He was affectionately named after her late husband, who died in World War II. Elvie was an optimistic lady who always chose to see the good in people — despite the tragedy of losing her beloved Roy. She always looked on the bright side of life but rarely ventured out into the world to try new things and meet new people.

One afternoon, she checked her mailbox and received some lottery scratch cards from what appeared to be a large corporation. She scratched the three panels and it read: "INSTANT WINNER OF $250,000." Elvie was dumbstruck. She immediately called the hotline number to excitedly declare herself a winner. The operator instructed her to send them her bank account details, and they would gladly send through the prize money.

Can you guess what happened next? Elvie sent them her bank account details. Within seven days the last $20,000 of her savings was drained in one of her accounts. It was a scam.

Elvie decided not to lose faith in humanity because of being swindled by a scam. She had other investments that could replace the loss. However, she decided to take the high road of consciousness and report the company by hiring a lawyer to investigate the operation. This was how she ended up meeting her new husband, James. Had her experience with the fake lottery not happened, she never would have ventured out of her comfort zone and then allowed love to enter her life. Elvie allowed the essence of trust in The Universe to prevail.

Dear Universe,

Allow me to fully trust in the circumstances I am presented with.
May I fully trust that everything I am currently experiencing is preparing me for what my soul has asked for.
So be it, so it is.

LAYLA GAVE BIRTH to a beautiful baby boy named Leo. He was around six weeks old when she went on her first trip to a shopping mall. Leo was a really happy baby who only woke up and got cranky when he wanted to eat. After shopping for 20 minutes, Layla found a table in the food court where she could rest and feed her baby. Because some people get a little freaked out by breastfeeding in public, she made sure that she was covered, but also that her baby could breathe.

"Can't you do that in the restroom please? My husband can see you doing that!" said a disgruntled woman from the next table.

"I'm feeding my son! Where would you have me go? Would you want to eat your sandwich in the toilet?" Layla replied.

Layla's tone was a little guarded (understandably), however she used it as an opportunity to educate the woman as to why it's so important not to feel ashamed of things that are perfectly natural. Her mission from that interaction was to normalize breastfeeding in public spaces for those who want to be out and about with their babies.

Remember

YES, IT'S IMPORTANT to be unashamed of who you are and what you're doing, as long as it's not intentionally harming others. However, your rules are not everyone's rules, so it's vital to hold compassion and normalize nature in order to avoid judgment.

Dear Universe,

May I release any shame or negativity from my energetic field. May I hold compassion for the viewpoints of others, but remain true to what I know to be natural. I am unashamed to express myself in the way that I need to as the beautiful human being that I am.

So be it, so it is.

92 UNIQUE

FEELING UNIQUE IS a fabulous manifestation. You wouldn't want to be "normal" or just like everyone else, would you? Hell, no! You are uniquely you! Just as no two snowflakes or fingerprints are the same, so, too, is the rare beauty of your soul that you bring to the world. When you feel unique, you can stand out from the crowd and create powerful and meaningful change.

Remember

THE TRUE GAME changers and visionaries in the world have an uncommon form of genius and way of expressing it. Everyone (without exception) has something unique to offer.

If you desire to manifest your own sense of uniqueness into the world, try this visualization in order to spark the magic of The Universe within you:

Imagine that you are sitting in front of a beautiful and ornate golden treasure chest. You pop the locks with your hand and it opens effortlessly. As the lid rises, you see a beautiful rose-colored glow from within the box. You peer in and see the biggest crystal you have ever seen in your life. Upon a second glance you realize it's one of the world's most coveted and rare gems ever discovered — a pink diamond found in the caves off the coast of Iceland. You can feel the healing, creative, and loving vibes radiating off that stone. What are other things you feel about it? Pause for a moment and write down three things that you feel from this vision.

Those three things are ultimately the unique aspects that you feel about yourself. The gem is YOU! There is only one in the world, and there is a sacred mission to fulfill.

Dear Universe,

May I embrace my own magnificence and uniqueness to fulfill my mission.
May I trust that I am not meant to be just like everyone else because that's not part of my divine plan to serve as a light worker in the world. Thank you for the awareness of who I truly am.
So be it, so it is.

---

93 | UPLIFTED

MANIFESTING THE FEELING of being uplifted can be so much fun. You need to ask yourself how you can create the perfect environment for fun, inspiration, and joy in every moment that you can. I like to teach my manifesting students to select something that I call a "Soul Song." It's a piece of music that you know will get you on a dance floor. Movement, especially through dance, is a fabulous way to feel uplifted and get the energy of happiness flowing.

Remember

THE MORE UPLIFTED you can feel, the better. Manifesting is all about seeking joy in the present moment, so the happier you feel, the more The Universe will deliver your desires into your life.

How can you share the love and make others feel more uplifted too? Can you share inspirational videos on social media? Could you commit a random act of kindness? There are infinite ways to help uplift people who need a little cheering up in the world. Make it your sacred soul mission to uplift others so that you feel uplifted.

Dear Universe,

Reveal to me ways that I can feel uplifted and then share that energy with others who need it right now. My heart is open to feeling as much joy as possible so I can raise my vibration and manifest my dreams and desires.
So be it, so it is.

---

94 VALUED

MANIFESTING THE ENERGY of feeling valued is important — it sparks so much joy. You don't want to ever feel as if you are not being appreciated or being taken for granted. However, in order to feel valued you must ask yourself, from a space of authenticity, if you are actually adding value to the lives of others. Are you valuable? Are you being of service? Are you contributing?

The entire Universe is based on a system of intention and feedback. This means that a request is sent out in energy form (vibration) and then mirrored back into our reality by The Universe (manifestation). On a personal level, it can be tricky to gauge your level of value if the people around you don't pause to comment on your efforts. For me, I've taught all four of my children to say "thank you" when someone does something for them. They look them in the eyes and take a moment to appreciate the person. The true meaning of "value" is to recognize the exchange of energy that has taken place.

Remember

VALUE YOURSELF FIRST. Also remember to appreciate others for the value they have contributed to your life. The expression of value is a mutual support system.

Recognition for being valued is vital, but you can't demand it. If you are truly coming from a space of service and commitment to excellence, then you trust that the energy you put out there will always return to you.

Dear Universe,

I ask that I feel valued by my friends, colleagues, and loved ones. I ask that I also take time to recognize others for their support in my life and take regular moments to appreciate their presence. Feeling valued motivates me to show up as the best version of myself.
So be it, so it is.

(95) VIBRANT

A VERY POWERFUL intention to hold in your heart is to live a vibrant life.

To feel vibrant you must eat healthy foods, partake in uplifting conversations, move your body, do things that you love, and surround yourself with the energy of happiness.

Remember

EVERYTHING IN THE Universe is energy and vibrating at a specific frequency. Affirm that you are feeling vibrant and high-energy, and your reality will be the manifestation of wellness.

For me, I believe that our favorite colors can help improve our moods — especially if they are vibrant colors. For years I have loved the color pink — it's been the soulful hued theme for my 30s. In my 20s, I was obsessed with purple, so who knows what my 40s' theme will be! The key point to remember is that any color that you love has the potential to make your heart sing. In my office, I have a vibrant pink orchid on my desk, a pink painting on the wall, pink sticky notes, pink highlighters, and of course my collection of rose quartz crystals on my manifestation altar.

Crystals are another excellent way to amplify your frequency so you feel more vibrant. When you're feeling vibrant, you're radiating a beautiful confidence that is uniquely yours. The Universe can play with your energy a lot more when you are in a state of feeling vibrant because you're open. Allow this to be your meditation to tune in to the vibrations around you and within your heart:

Dear Universe,

My life is extremely vibrant. My energy speaks louder than my words and I am devoted to nurturing my frequency in order to attract what my heart truly dreams and desires. Everything is energy and I am committed to being a high-vibe individual who manifests magic.

So be it, so it is.

VISIBLE

ALLOWING YOURSELF TO be visible can be somewhat confronting. However, if you want to make a difference in the world and authentically connect with others, then you must allow yourself to be seen.

My man, Sean, and I tried something once which we called "Soul Gazing": We stared into one another's eyes for as long as possible.

The process was a lot tougher and intimate than I ever could have imagined. At first, we were both laughing and found it tough to settle. I was fidgeting, not able to keep still or keep my eyes locked with Sean's; they would flit all over the place. But then we both started to really "see" one another, and I'm talking about the type of seeing where you can see the fabric of spirit starting to twinkle in tiny particles that transform you. We forged through various stages ranging from laughter, playfulness, curiosity, and then tears.

It was the most vulnerable I have ever been with another human being — he could see ALL of me. What was the biggest surprise was how much of a wall I had created around this level of intimacy. We had dabbled with it in the past, but hadn't consciously made time for it. How hard can it be to truly stare into someone's eyes?

Remember

A NEW LEVEL of compassion and connectedness is unlocked when you allow yourself to be visible.

Life is all about peeling back the layers to uncover a new level of consciousness and connection to the divine within. I would highly recommend that you try this exercise with someone you love and trust and begin with this as your meditation:

Dear Universe,

I am open to being completely visible and seen by other people. There is no need to hide or build a wall around my heart. I am safe, I am seen. With this understanding, I am able to thrive.
So be it, so it is.

97 VULNERABLE

THE ABILITY TO be vulnerable with someone is indeed magical. It opens doorways to hearts that were initially closed. It also builds trust and creates space for a strong connection and friendship to be established.

Remember

IF YOU ARE willing to be vulnerable with others, you ignite the magic of humanity and miraculous collaboration.

My soulful honor with the work that I do in the world is to be brave enough to be vulnerable. I remember the first time I spoke onstage at a women's networking event, sharing the story of leaving my ten-year marriage of domestic violence. I felt nervous to the pit of my stomach, but I knew that if I didn't suck it up and get over myself, I couldn't help anyone. There were around 200 women in the room. As I told my story, I sensed so much emotional feedback from the audience. I could see eyes were filling with tears, hands were held on hearts, and we were all engaged in a soulful dialogue about the power of change.

Many months later, a woman who was in that audience sent me an email saying that she had finally built the courage to leave her 20-year abusive marriage because of hearing me speak. From that day forward I have held the belief that vulnerability has the power to radically change lives, and we each have a responsibility to our fellow humans to lead with love.

Dear Universe,

Allow me to share experiences from within my heart
from a space of vulnerability. Although it might seem scary
at first, I trust that sharing my journey and my truth will help
illuminate a path of healing for someone in need.
So be it, so it is.

WELCOMED

NOTHING IS SWEETER than feeling like you are welcomed by loved ones or friends. Expectant parents spend months preparing for the arrival of their newborn so that the child feels loved and welcomed into their home. When a family member arrives home from a trip, people tend to make "welcome home" signs.

Remember

MAKING OTHERS FEEL welcomed in your life or in your home is a great way to strengthen friendships and relationships. It opens your heart and creates space for kindness to manifest.

In America, when someone says "thank you," the other person replies with "you're welcome." It took me the longest time to feel genuine when I said that. In Australia, if someone says thank you, people say nothing, or "my pleasure," or "it's okay," or "no worries." When I first moved to Las Vegas, hearing people say "you're welcome" felt so disingenuous. Now I see it as a vital part of American culture. It's the completion of a cycle of an exchange of kindness. Welcoming people is a gesture of opening your heart — and the world will always need more of this kind of energy.

Dear Universe,

May I feel welcomed wherever I go. May I also make others feel welcomed in my home and in my company. This opens the flow of connection between myself and my near and dear ones. Thank you, Universe, for the awareness of including people in my life. It fuels my heart and feels so good.
So be it, so it is.

99 WHOLE

YOU HAVE EVERYTHING you need right now. You are enough. You are complete. You will always be on a miraculous journey of love, of light, and of growth.

Remember

TRUE CONTENTMENT, TRUE peace, and true embodiment of wholeness is the manifestation of who you are right now and will always be.

If you find yourself wanting something, feeling like you need more, feeling like something is missing — remember, it is your intuition calling you to expand. It's not The Universe telling you that you are not whole, because you already are and you already have been.

Today's society (and particularly the media) has been designed to help us feel not good enough. Sales are generated because we don't feel whole. However, when you shift to a space of mindfulness, you can get off the crazy treadmill of limiting beliefs and refuse to get stuck in the cycle any longer.

You are part of the wholeness of reality, of The Universe, of existence. You are part of all that is and has ever been since the dawn of time. Make it your daily affirmation to remember that you are enough, you are worthy, and you are whole. You are complete in your imperfection — as we all are. You are complete in your presence.

The collective consciousness of The Universe deeply appreciates you for being here.

Dear Universe,

Thank you for the perspective of seeing the wholeness of the energetic field of potential. May I always feel whole. In moments when I feel a little empty, may I be reminded that I am a proud representative, manifestation, and energy of your consciousness.
So be it, so it is.

WORTHY

FEELING WORTHY IS your birthright because you are a beautiful human being. We all have faults, flaws, quirks, regrets, mistakes, and spiritual detours, and this makes us perfect in the imperfection.

I've worked with thousands of people over the years to help them to manifest their dreams. I would say that the number 1 theme that stops someone from living an intentional life of greatness is not feeling worthy. You might question yourself, doubt your desires, or not want to be more successful than people in your family.

Your worth is to be cherished and treasured — like a rare and exotic flower that you must feed and water in your mind's eye on a moment-by-moment basis.

Remember

YOU MUST LEARN to silence the tiny voice in your heart that tells you that you are not enough.

The Universe has seeded this whisper into your consciousness as a challenge to rise above and remember that you are worthy. It's your call to step into your power and engage in the energy of compassion and kindness for yourself. Also, learning how to receive is imperative in cultivating your feelings of worthiness. Instead of rejecting compliments, stating that a gift is "too much," or not asking for help, remember to love yourself fiercely and feel worthy. Why? Because you are. You always have been worthy and you always will be.

Dear Universe,

I am connected to the core essence of my soul. I remember that I am worthy of anything my heart desires. I am enough. I now stand guard at the doorway to my thinking and reject critical thoughts that question my worth. As my worthiness strengthens, I have more to give to others.
So be it, so it is.

Part 4:

KEEPING UP THE MOMENTUM OF INSPIRATION

The
10 Foundational
Elements *of*
Manifestation *to*
Remember

W hen you are on this incredible adventure with The Universe, it's important to make sure that you can keep the momentum of inspiration alive and spark the energy of remembering. To do this you must "remember" the following ten foundational elements that will support you on your journey to manifesting.

1. *Remember:* YOU ARE ALWAYS WORKING, PLAYING, AND FLOWING WITH THE UNIVERSE.

There is no separation between yourself and the Oneness of all life and the energy that animates every single atom in the fabric of the cosmos. Everything that exists is governed by the highest energy of them all. Call it God, Source, The Force, The Universe, or whatever you feel comfortable with. The Universe is the oscillation of the highest vibration of love and superconsciousness. You are The Universe and an expression of that same energy. With this awareness, you will remember your power to create your own reality.

2. *Remember:* YOU MUST BELIEVE THAT ANYTHING IS POSSIBLE.

You must hold the belief very close to your heart that everything and anything is possible — even (and especially) if it defies all logic. You must learn how to believe beyond what you can see and detach from "how" something will manifest. Being open to all possibilities opens you up to the opportunity for miracles to appear in your reality.

3. *Remember:* YOU NEED TO LEARN HOW TO TRUST AND SURRENDER IN THE PROCESS OF MANIFESTATION.

Once an intention or a desire has been released to The Universe, for the Law of Attraction to work magic you must learn how to guide your energy and trust in the process. Surrender is not the same as quitting — it's learning how to manage your energy and to not create resistance around your intention, which blocks it from appearing in your reality. As the old saying goes, "a watched pot never boils" — so distraction also works wonders. To do this, you might wish to find something to take your attention away from looking for results or signs or evidence of your desires manifesting. For instance, watch a TV show, go for a walk, paint a picture, cook a meal, learn a new language —

anything that will get you out of your head and into the space of trusting that The Universe is mapping out the details in perfect divine timing.

4. *Remember:* THE ENERGY YOU PUT OUT THERE WILL ALWAYS COME BACK TO YOU.

When you understand the Law of Attraction, you know that whatever energy you are willing to put out there will always boomerang its way back to you. The awareness to remember is to only radiate energy that you're willing to have echoed back to you by The Universe. Our entire existence is a giant mirror that reflects back to us what we need to learn in order to grow as human beings.

5. *Remember:* USE THE AFFIRMATION "THIS OR SOMETHING BETTER."

There are many different ways The Universe delivers your desires. One step in the process that is often overlooked is that you always attract what you are ready for. Sometimes this brings with it a sense of disappointment that your manifestation isn't exactly what you ordered. When this feeling arises, try and meditate on the feeling that The Universe is always manifesting things in perfect, divine timing, in the highest order for your greater good. Sometimes what you want isn't what your soul needs in order to thrive and grow. Your higher self knows and trusts that you are always on the right path.

6. *Remember:* YOUR WORD IS YOUR WAND.

Being on the manifesting journey requires you to master your language patterns and the words you choose to use. The emotions that accompany your words are the energetic essence of what fuels your manifestations. Simply put, your thoughts are electric and your emotions are magnetic.

When you bring awareness to your language patterns, you tend to become hyperaware of words and phrases that don't serve you any longer. Avoiding the use of the word "hate," or universals such as "always," "every," and "never," helps to keep your vibration open to all miraculous possibilities and disengage from magnetizing those words emotionally. Your words hold tremendous power in sculpting your future path. Empowering words will take you higher, whereas words fueled by limiting beliefs will keep you small. The blessing is that you get to choose.

7. *Remember:* PRACTICE THE ART OF GRATITUDE.

If you remember to feel thankful for everything that shows up in your reality, no matter what it is, then you are creating space for The Universe to manifest more magic and miracles into your life. Even saying thank you for the smallest manifestation will raise your vibration and clear the way for bigger and more magnificent things to appear.

Make sure you write down three things that you are grateful for at the end of each day. This will help send your subconscious mind a magical boost before you sleep at night. This magnetic energy of appreciation can commune with The Universe and send out a signal that you are ready and willing to receive more things to be grateful for.

8. *Remember:* KEEP GOOD COMPANY AND FIND YOUR SOUL TRIBE.

When you surround yourself with people who inspire you and support you on your journey, you can share the emotions that unfold on the adventure. Finding like-minded, kindred spirits to surround yourself with will help keep your energy high and your heart full. We are the energetic sum of the top five people we spend the most time with. If you're not able to connect with like-minded people in your community, then please consider setting an intention to attract them into your reality.

Check out my Manifesting Academy (manifestingacademy.com) and learn about becoming part of my exclusive Soul Tribe. It's a space to share your manifesting journey and make lifelong friends.

9. *Remember:* MONEY IS ENERGY.

People who don't have issues with money tend to find it easy to manifest abundance. They don't believe it to be the "root of all evil" — in fact they love it like it's a good friend because they take care of it. They send it lots of love, and it usually tends to multiply because money is energy. Money is the expressed consciousness of The Universe for the act of service. Anything that you send love to will expand — money is no different.

10. *Remember:* SET POWERFUL INTENTIONS AND FOCUS ON HOW YOU FEEL.

People who are great at manifesting open up space to regularly map out a clear path for what they really want to create in their lives. They know (without a shadow of a doubt) that manifesting requires time to design the details with unique specificity. They turn it into a fun game with The Universe and trust that their desires will show up in divine timing.

Intention setting is a safe and sacred space for love to always rise above fear in order for you to dream big. Whether you want to be a published author or a croquet champion, land your soulmate, or be a super-present parent . . . the rules of this game are simple:

- Get clear about what you want.
- Write it down.
- Work toward it physically (taking inspired action) and energetically (guiding your emotions).
- See/feel it as if it has already happened. Feel grateful.

SPARKING THE ESSENCE OF VISUALIZATION

Geneviève Behrend, born in 1881, was an author and teacher of New Thought who lived in New York. She desired to travel to Cornwall in England to study with a new spiritual teacher, but she didn't have the money to do so. Every night and morning she visualized counting out twenty $1,000 bills. This was much more money than she actually needed, but it helped her to tune in to the energy of limitless possibilities. In her mind's eye she would picture buying her ticket to London, then traveling on the ship, and then ultimately sitting with her new teacher and how that would feel.

Geneviève's affirmation was this: "My mind is a center of divine operations." It took about six weeks for her to manifest the money that was needed.

As a powerful creator, you must take time to visualize your goals, dreams, wishes, and desires. There are so many reasons that a vision board is an effective strategy to strengthen your connection to The Universe and to also gain clarity about what you really want to create in your life. The key component is to allow yourself to feel the emotions connected to the imagery and trinkets you choose to place on your board. It shouldn't be all about stuff and material possessions, because the more you focus on how you feel, the more that energy expands. It's your experience and feeling of owning a brand-new Tesla, not necessarily the Tesla itself.

Here's an example. In 2013, my love, Sean, and I were planning our wedding. We were living in Australia at the time, but we were going to celebrate our special day at a boutique hotel in Las Vegas. I decided to create a vision board with certain elements that I loved and felt inspired by to construct the energy of my special day. In the middle of the board, I placed a beautiful picture of a bouquet of peonies. As I glued the image to the board, I felt and visualized how it would feel to be walking down the aisle, with my father, toward my new husband — the love of my life.

I knew I wanted to have peonies as my bridal bouquet. When the time came to call the florist to order the flowers, I was so saddened to hear that peonies were not in season that time of year and it would be virtually impossible to order them within my budget. I ordered a different type of flower (roses) and just accepted that my vision wasn't going to manifest.

The key here is to TRUST the process as it unfolds and affirm: "This or something better." Going with the flow releases the resistance from what you truly wish to manifest.

The day of the wedding, the florist made a mistake and delivered the wrong flowers to the event. They called me and apologized profusely for delivering a bouquet of peonies instead of roses! It was the exact arrangement of peonies that I had on my vision board MONTHS earlier — even the same color!

The Universe will deliver what we have imprinted into our subconscious mind because it's always conspiring to build our reality around how we feel. It's not up to us to understand "how" something will manifest; we just have to trust that everything will unfold in perfect divine timing.

HOW TO CREATE YOUR VISION BOARD

The best way to create a vision board is to gather your supplies intuitively. Select images from a stack of magazines/brochures/junk mail and also cut out words that activate an emotional response within your heart. You could also add things like oracle cards, quotations, bookmarks, feathers, stickers, or even glitter — whatever gets you into that feeling space of inspiration. Place and glue everything onto a large piece of poster board.

When you create your vision board, make sure that you will be alone for an hour or so. Pour yourself a glass of wine or brew up a cup of green tea, switch off your phone, and relax into this joyful process. Music can also be helpful to inspire the magic of this creative activity.

See in your mind's eye your ideal lifestyle. Immerse yourself into the feeling space of gratitude in the present moment as if your desires have already manifested. The power of now is the pivotal point of creation. Remember: There are no rules! You can create the board however you feel inspired to do so. You can even create multiple boards for different intentions if you wish.

Once your board is complete, place it somewhere so that you will see it often. You could even take a photo of it and have it as your desktop screensaver or phone background. This way the images sink into your mind on a regular basis.

If you want to gain clarity about what you would like to manifest in your life and how you intend to feel, please download this free gift I created for you at SarahProut.com/gift. The Universe responds better when you are clear about what you desire to be, do, and have in your life.

DESIGN YOUR SACRED SPACE

Now that you have your vision board and you've set powerful intentions, it's important to create other sacred spaces in your home to support your adventure. Creating an altar is a magical way to spark a conversation with The Universe in your home or office. You can meditate with your altar, use affirmations or mantras, or spend time visualizing what you want to create. It amplifies your intention and your frequency. It also supports sacred space for your desires to manifest. An altar is not just for decoration and to look pretty, but contains items that help you maintain focus, inspiration, and a powerful flow of energy. As a spiritual space, you want to make sure that it accurately represents what you believe in.

It can be such a fun project to create an altar in your home. Make sure it's in a quiet space that will be undisturbed by people. The last thing you want is children or guests asking questions about the trinkets that you energetically charge with your own magic. Also, it must only be touched by you or your beloved — of course with your permission.

Some ideas of what to put on your altar include:

- Crystals (rose quartz for love, citrine for abundance)
- Candles (colors and scents that inspire an essence of wonder)
- Icons and statues: I have a Lakshmi statue, which is the Hindu Goddess of Abundance. My husband, Sean, has a really cool statue of Merlin the wizard. Find the deities or icons that mean something to you.
- Journal: You could place a gratitude journal or a notebook on your altar. This amplifies your intentions.
- Essential oils: The plant magic of essential oils dates back to ancient Egyptian times. Associating your intentions to a scent will help to anchor them in your subconscious mind.
- Sage: Burning sage helps clear the energy. (You can buy sage at Whole Foods or find it on Amazon.)
- Oracle or inspiration cards
- Flowers: Fresh flowers are a wonderful way to keep the energy of your altar alive and vibrant.
- Special books (Hint: you could place your copy of *Dear Universe* on your altar and share a photo on Instagram. Use the hashtag #DearUniverse.)
- Jewelry: Keep any trinkets of special mementos on your altar to infuse it with powerful energy — mala beads, lockets, symbolic pieces.

The intention is to collect and curate your altar with items that you find dear to your heart and that mean something to you. They are sacred reminders that you are working with The Universe to create your own reality.

DAILY RITUALS FOR CONNECTION

In order to keep the momentum of inspiration flowing, you must create daily rituals to connect with The Universe and to your intentions. These could be things such as acts of self-care like taking a warm bath, reading an inspirational book, playing games with your loved ones, visualizing your intention, or taking five minutes to meditate. In fact, meditation is the foundational element of maintaining your connection, which is why the mini-meditations in this book are so powerful.

Did you know that meditation can help you release the emotional blocks that are holding you back from manifesting your desires? We live in this beautiful Universe where everything is energy, and yet we forget the power we have to tap into our own limitless potential unless we schedule it into our busy daily lives. Studies show that people who meditate regularly have physiological ages 12 to 15 years less than their actual age. This is why it's so important to tune in to the energy of The Universe through the daily practice of meditation.

SHARE YOUR "DEAR UNIVERSE" MOMENTS

The final element of keeping the momentum of inspiration is to share what inspires you, to pay the energy forward.

If the stories or mini-meditations throughout this book have resonated within your heart, I would dearly love for you to share some of your "Dear Universe" moments with me (and also your friends and family), if you feel called to do so. There are many ways to work with me and connect on social media (@sarahprout) and on my website, SarahProut.com.

The process of bringing *Dear Universe* to life is the manifestation of a life-long dream for me. My intention is that the message and teachings within this book will inspire you to pass them on — to share what you feel inspired by. Let's create a movement together where we can help others rise above fear, embrace love, and remember the power we have to instantly manifest a "Dear Universe" moment of transformation.

From my soul to yours, I deeply honor you for being on this journey with me.

With love and gratitude,

Sarah Prout xo

Acknowledgments

GRATITUDE.

Heartfelt thanks and endless gratitude to my editor, Justin Schwartz, and the team at HMH for believing in me. Special thanks to Katelyn Morse for the beautiful illustrations.

To my agents at Sterling Lord Literistic: Jaidree Braddix and Celeste Fine, you are incredible. Thank you for sparking the magic of this journey.

Sean Patrick Simpson, I love you, and I see you. You are the love of my life, my mirror. You are my greatest manifestation, and I'm so grateful to be on this wild adventure with you.

Thomas Anthony, Olivia Rose, Lulu Dawn, and Ava Moon — thank you for being here. Words cannot express how much joy you have blessed my heart with. You are all amazing, brilliant, and beautiful human beings — I am so honored to be your mother.

Tony Prout and Louise Findlay, I love you both so much.

Big hugs and eternal thanks to my dear friends Dallyce Brisbin and Scott deMoulin.

Giant waves of gratitude to the entire team at Soul Space Media, especially Kim West, Mavi Barrena, and Jon Marino. To our customers, Manifesting Academy students, Soul Tribe members, SarahProut.com readers, Journey to Manifesting podcast listeners, subscribers, and fans: your support means the world to me and you inspire me with your stories of hope, transformation, and insight.

To my family, friends, soul family, and mentors: I adore you all! Lauren and Roger Simpson, Bree Argetsinger and Bodhi, Grace Smith, Bernardo Smith-Feitosa, Marla Mattenson, Kris Britton, Ryan Yokome, Bronya Wilkins, Amber Petty, Rebecca Lange, Cathy and Gemma Penglase, Alyce Pilgrim, John Ronaldo Brans, Samuel Hawley, Henrietta Prout, David Fraser, Reuben Crossman, Vishen Lakhiani, Miriam Gobovic, Klemen Struc, Mindvalley.com, DigitalMarketer.com, Shelly Lefkoe, Andrea Lee, Jess Tomlinson, Joan Georgina, Betsy Green, Mary Veronica Diedrich, Kirpal Singh Ji Gill, Joy Patterson. There are literally hundreds of names to mention and thank. You know who you are!

Thanks to "Max" — without the tumultuous nature of our ten years together, this book would not have been possible. Our story has empowered and inspired many people and I am so grateful.

Last but not least, extra special thanks to The Universe for the magical and beautiful adventure called life that flows through each and every one of us.

Resources

DEAR UNIVERSE — THE ONLINE EXPERIENCE

The key to success is to find the right support on your journey to manifesting. Here is a list of various resources intended to spark the magic of limitless possibilities and to continue your *Dear Universe* adventure.

THE GIFT

Download your FREE *Dear Universe* Intention Setting Worksheet. This will help you gain clarity on how you desire to feel in your life and what you want to manifest. Access it from SarahProut.com/gift.

THE BOOK CLUB

This is more than just a book club — this is about your journey through the 200 mini-meditations in *Dear Universe* and sharing your experience with others. We'll have real conversations about rising above fear, embracing love, and remembering your power. Learn more at SarahProut.com/bookclub.

THE VISUALIZATION

Dear Universe guides you through your emotions, and when combined with this visualization, you will connect with an imagined future version of yourself. Spark this sacred conversation with The Universe to catch a glimpse of who you are and who you will become in the near future. Access it from SarahProut.com/visualization.

CONNECT WITH SARAH PROUT

I adore being in touch with my readers and fans. Here's how to connect with me:

Facebook: You can connect with me at @LoveSarahProut. I especially love Instagram, too — @SarahProut. Make sure you use the hashtag #DearUniverse to share the mini-meditations that resonate in your heart.

SarahProut.com: There are hundreds of free articles to inspire your manifesting adventures.

Email: Send your *Dear Universe* moments to hello@sarahprout.com.

Podcast: It's called Journey to Manifesting, and the intention is to inspire you to create the life of your wildest dreams. New episodes are released weekly.

INDEX